A New F

for

Exceptional Living

M.♦.R.E.

A New Philosophy
for
Exceptional Living

M.O.R.E.

MOVEMENT

EXCEPTION · OPPORTUNITY

REALITY

Alyson Jones, MA

Book Design: Marla Thompson
Typesetting: Greg Salisbury
Portrait Photographer: Lee Halliday

This book is dedicated with deepest love and gratitude to the members of my exceptional family who have supported me in living a life of passion and purpose. To my husband Bruce who has kept his promise and is my true love, my twins Aidan and Bronwyn who made me believe in magic again, my nephew and niece, Leif and Kiara, who helped me see a bigger picture in life, my brother Darwyn who has shared a lifetime of fun and celebration with me, and my mother Sonja who built the foundation for us all.

Testimonials

"Alyson Jones is a highly respected therapist, educator and author who has practiced for over 20 years and worked with all age groups. This knowledge has given her a unique perspective as an author. Unlike any other self-help book, she cuts through to the truth and holds up a mirror for the reader to reflect on their own life."
Joyce Taylor-Bauers, President of Taylor Made Media

"Frank, direct and clear in her message, Alyson articulates a common sense, realistic approach to living an exceptional life. Her message demonstrates that an exceptional life is not the luxury of a few, but is accessible to all."
Tracy Theemes, Financial Advisor, Sophia Financial Group, Raymond James LtdAuthor, The Financially Empowered Woman

"Living a life that is full and meaningful is a universal human desire. Alyson Jones' book is unlike any other self-help book. Practical in her approach, offering clarity, honesty and realism, she shows readers how lives can be lived to their fullest potential."
Erle Dardick, CEO, MonkeyMedia Software
Author of Get Catering and Grow Sales!

"As the era of wanting more is exploding around us, Alyson Jones creates an essential distinction as she reframes the MORE we have been searching for. In her practical and useful book, Alyson provides a simple philosophy, rich and relatable personal stories, and questions for self reflection that will help you get MORE for your exceptional life."
Tana Heminsley, CEO and Founder, Authentic Leadership Global™
Author, Awaken Your Authentic Leadership

Acknowledgements

It is with deep gratitude that I acknowledge all the people who have inspired, impacted, provoked, and supported me along my path.

First of all, I would like to thank the many families, parents, and youth who have allowed me into their lives as a consultant and therapist. You have been my greatest teachers. I have experienced beautiful moments of breakthrough with you as well as humbling moments when I missed the mark. Each of you has taught me dignity in my mistakes as well as my successes. Your openness, courage, and trust have inspired me. It is here that I wish I could name names but I cannot; so I honour each and every one of you in this manner. Thank you.

Thank you to my professional network that has supported and believed in me through the years. I have been blessed to cross paths with so many exceptional people who are truly making an impact in this world. From my fellow therapists to the legal and financial specialists I have met throughout the years: thank you for sharing your knowledge and expertise with me, and for teaching me how to work in an inter-disciplinary team. Thank you to Dr. Gordon Neufeld who has inspired me professionally and as a parent, and has facilitated many summer intensives in which I have truly been able to dig deeper into understanding my self and my family.

To the many people who taught me about business and leadership, your assistance has been of such value to my life. Thank you to Susan Roberts who changed my world when she gave me my first real counselling job, and the dear friends who have become my compatriots in this journey, long after our time together at Cameray Counselling Center. My gratitude also to Sandy Gerber who helped me define the MORE philosophy and understand how this has always been my driving force, and to my Thrive Sisterhood of women leaders who brought the fun to business. Thank you to Tracy Theemes who provides one of the best reality checks I know, and to those many others who have showed me how to bring my visions to reality.

To my colleagues and students at the Adler School of Professional Psychology, thank you for allowing me to be a part of a respectful and innovative educational organization. I feel honoured to be among the faculty. A special thank you to Dr. Larry Axelrod for giving me the opportunity to share my ideas with the young minds in our field, and also to my students who have fueled me in countless ways.

To Angela Kelman and my Monday night singing group "The Grown Up Girls", sharing our stories and our voices has energized me just when I needed it. Thank you all for cheering me on as I wrote this book.

Thank you to my publisher Julie Salisbury, Gulnar Patel, Nina Shoroplova, and the rest of the team at Influence Publishing. Julie walked me step-by-step through this process with humour, joy, and encouragement. Thank you to the editing team at Influence Publishing for helping me understand that good editing helps to makes a good book better. You have all provided me with the opportunity and the vehicle to put MORE to action.

To my team of Associates at Alyson Jones & Associates, you are truly bringing MORE to the table and I am thrilled to be sharing this experience with you. A big thanks to my administration team that makes things happen, and are the backbone of my vision. Kim Erickson you are a ray of sunshine!

It is with such joy that I thank my friends and extended family. What an amazing group of people I have in my life. There are too many of you to name, but I am grateful to each and every one of you. You know who you are and my heart is filled with gratitude for your presence in my life.

A special thank you to Nancy Brown. You have always had my back and put out fires on more than one occasion. I am deeply grateful to have you in my life as a business manager (yes you are a true Admin Ninja), a facilitator, and most of all as a friend. Everything is better when you are a part of it!

To my mother Sonja Jones who was the first editor in my life, and somehow managed to read and edit every paper and essay through my school years: you taught me to love reading and to value books as part of the fabric of life.

And finally thank you to my immediate family for supporting me and allowing me the space and time to write this book. My husband Bruce who did the early edits and has always believed in me: you and I are on a wonderful journey together, and I could not have a better partner than you on this journey. Thank you to my children, Aidan and Bronwyn, who have always inspired me and opened my heart to a whole new level of life experience. To my nephew Leif and niece Kiara: you have added such spark and excitement to this life. When I started the book I hoped it would be of benefit to others, but it has become my deepest wish that my children will read this book and understand a few of those "life lessons" I am trying to pass on. I believe in you all and I know you are each exceptional in your own beautiful and unique way. You are all my greatest joys and in the end, this book is for you!

Contents

Prologue

Welcome to MORE. I am pleased to act as your guide throughout this book. Life can be complicated; this is a guidebook to offer proven strategies and approaches to assist you along your journey.

The title of this book–MORE–is an acronym standing for "Movement, Opportunity, Reality, and Exception." Together, these four principles comprise the tools that can assist each of us in living an exceptional life.

When it comes to explaining why I chose to write this particular book, as well as describing how it may be helpful to you—there is both good and bad news. It would appear that I am qualified to write this book, as I am a Professional Therapist who has been working in the field of Psychology and Parent Education for years. Yes, that is both the good news and the bad news!

The good news is that I have gained cumulative insights through many years of professional practice. On many occasions, clients have been kind enough, and patient enough, to allow me to try out my different theories and ideas on them. I am actually tried, true, and tested. On the other hand, the bad news is that I am, by virtue of my placement in the category of "helping professional," in a field that tends to confuse its users.

Counselling has unfortunately taken on a bad rap in the general population. Many people envision counselling as the end result of some sort of problem-based experience, in which they recline on a couch and talk about their past. The entertainment industry loves to characterize and portray this aspect of therapy, right down to the stoic counsellor saying, "How do you feel about that?" The client lays on a well-upholstered sofa, or at the very least sits on a large comfy chair, and talks endlessly about his or her feelings or past. In these characterizations, the therapist is a dispassionate, neutral being who asks occasional questions and shares academic-sounding insights. This is not my experience of counselling, nor would I think my clients would describe anything close to these circumstances—except for the fact that

I have some comfortable furniture that I prefer they not lie on!

What is counselling and why should people care that I am a counsellor? Why should anybody listen to me, and of what value is this book? All valid questions, but the answers might not be quite what you expect. I am approaching teaching the philosophy of MORE in the same way I approach my counselling practice, as an authentic person who is also a professional. This book will interweave stories from my practice and my life, while defining a core philosophy and the steps to exceptional living.

But first it helps for the reader to understand a little about my profession and why it is relevant that I am a professional in this field. Psychology is a field that draws curious and compassionate people. Most counsellors truly want to help others in some capacity. This is a good thing, but there are times when abstract thinkers are filled with the best of intentions, but are a bit short on practical applications. It is my commitment to bring forth the vision, and to do so in a way that is practical and based on common sense.

In order to understand why my guidance can be of assistance to my reader, I introduce a very brief history of the counselling field. The psychiatric-medical model was the beginning of professional psychology. This model is often described as having a large gap between the therapist and the person seeking assistance. In this model, the subject is termed a "patient" rather than a "client," and there is potential for a power dynamic in the relationship between the therapist and the "patient." In addition, the medical model brings a focus to the pathology of the "patient." As originally conceived, the psychiatric-medical model contributed greatly to understanding human behaviours and has helped many people along the way. The model also has a large body of academic research attached to it that provides a solid basis under the field of Psychology. As a professional in the psychological field I am aware of this research, so my perspective is well informed and substantiated, and this has directly benefited the people I have worked with through the years.

As psychology developed, a movement emerged that addressed the power dynamic: the counsellor began operating from a place of unconditional positive regard for the person seeking therapy. In the non-directive model of therapy the "patient" became the "client." At the core of this optimistic model of therapy is respect for the client and a trust that, given the right environment and circumstance, people have the capacity to heal themselves. On the downside, this non-directive model of therapy has been known to leave some clients feeling that they have spoken to a nice person, but that they have not received a lot of practical help. This "talk" might have been a pleasant experience, but it might also fall short of some people's expectations. Although I do positively regard my clients and believe in their capacity to heal, I also feel an obligation to provide common sense information and practical strategies for life solutions, and that is the same approach I bring to this book.

As counselling professionals, we are currently attempting to define ourselves and help others understand the relevancy of counselling in our modern world. We have a society filled with very busy, potentially stressed people who want concrete results to compensate for their time and commitment and do not want to be stigmatized by seeking therapy and having to go to the "head shrinker."

It is my belief that counselling can provide a much-needed service in our modern world, but counsellors need to grow and adapt with the times. As I have never figured out the secrets of "head shrinking," this book is also designed to assist people in understanding that effective guidance has nothing to do with either voodoo or detached academics. This book seeks to demystify the self-help counselling world and provide the reader with true value for their time and money. In addition, this book maintains respect for the reader and strives to deliver a practical framework from which each reader can assess what is relevant and beneficial to them.

Now I do have a warning for my readers and those who are seeking assistance. There are many very good therapists and coaches, but like any profession, they range from the adequate to the truly exceptional. To complicate things further and truly confuse the general population, there are also "counsellors" and "coaches" who have no professional affiliations or standardized training. There has been a huge rise in "life coaching" and, as many people feel more comfortable with the term "coaching" instead of the term "counselling", this field is flourishing. The coaching profession is maturing and evolving, and becoming increasingly professional, but the consumer of "life coaching" services has to be careful that they are dealing with somebody substantial rather than a flaky "wannabe." There are a whole slew of people out there who call themselves counsellors and coaches, and who assert that they can heal the world because they were somehow healed, but life experience does not immediately qualify one to work as a professional in this field. If you or someone you know is using the services of a life coach or counsellor, make sure the service provider has jumped through the appropriate professional hoops. The reader can rest assured that I have done my fair share of hoop-jumping and that the information in this book is both substantial and practical.

Another related and worrisome trend is that professional counselling and therapy has become confused and enmeshed with the self-help genre. Although there are many excellent books aimed at self-growth and development, common sense and discernment are needed when sorting through all the material that is out there. The self-help field is saturated and the quality of information provided can vary tremendously from book to book. There are many people who read self-help books who associate psychology and the "helping" professions with insubstantial and unsatisfactory "fluff." Please do not consider this to be a "fluffy-be-happy" self-help book. It is my purpose and goal that this book be useful, thought-provoking and motivating for the reader and I would much rather be your guide on the journey than approach you as if you need "help"; all you may need is a few pointers along the way. I have always felt bothered by the lack of practical information in many self-help books. I'd rather not contribute to the plethora of material that I sometimes feel is doing more damage than service—that ever-growing, ever-annoying, and all-knowing group who believe you need to be helped and that they have all the answers.

Although I have noted some concerns about the helping professions, I want to make it clear that there is significant value in counselling, psychological literature, and modern psychology. In order to be creative in our lives we need to understand ourselves, and it is my intent that this guide book provide an effective path for personal development. People are endlessly interesting and it follows that it is good to be interested in your life.

So why is this book aimed at offering you practical steps to a life philosophy?

Let us consider that the "core" of a philosophy is where it all starts and if an individual does not spend sufficient time building a strong and solid foundation, life tends to collapse. We all know that a house with a strong foundation can withstand some severe elements, but a quickly built, insubstantial structure can blow away in the wind. There is a lot of truth in the analogy of "The Three Little Pigs" and my intent is to assist you in having a well-built house when the storm comes.

The more clarity we have regarding our philosophy of life and our core values, the more likely we are to achieve our goals and live a successful and satisfying life. This book is designed to benefit your understanding of the life you have and to help you make the most of it.

The subject that is at the heart of this book is my "core" philosophy of life; that "core" is MORE.

M Movement
O Opportunity
R Reality
E Exception

The acronym "MORE" stands for the essential words: "Movement, Opportunity, Reality, and Exception." These propel my life and my professional practice. I have developed this "core" philosophy throughout my years of practice and living life. No matter the circumstance or the issue in front of me, I have found that this philosophy gives me the solid framework from which I can build something exceptional.

Let's break it down. Basically we are talking about a methodology I have developed for living in the moment. No matter what situation is in front of me, I run through my list of core words, "Movement, Opportunity, Reality, and Exception", to look for insight about how the situation might be enhanced for the best interests of all concerned.

First, I look for circumstances or challenges that need to move; second, I assess the opportunities in front of me; third, I observe the reality of the situation; and fourth, I commit to a path where the first three factors can lead to something exceptional.

In order for this book to be authentic and to present my core philosophy of MORE, it will require that I share intimate parts of my story. It would not be possible to write this particular book solely from a professional and detached place. To be real, I need to write from a place of balance between my personal and professional lives. As a counsellor, teacher, and presenter, there have always been specific professional boundaries set up as part of my interactions with others. There is more to me; and I am ready to share the parts of me that have previously been kept more private. In other words, to write an interesting book about an exceptional life, it is necessary to expose what I consider to be my exceptional life.

If this book is to be real and true to me, as well as useful to you, it cannot be flaky. It needs to be concrete, practical, and straightforward with a goal to be of service to those who choose to read it. I want to shake you up a little and encourage you to see the possibilities in your own life through the philosophy of MORE.

We all have blocks that get in our way. Each and every human being has strengths and challenges. One person may be lost in procrastination, whereas another may wear blinders, not choosing to see the truth in their life. Although there are central themes and patterns in all human behaviour, our personal blocks are different. This book is not intended to address all the problems that bog us down or why we have them, but rather to take the material we have in our individual lives, turn it on high, and make it exceptional through the MORE philosophy.

CHAPTER ONE

The Philosophy of Exceptional Living; Preparing For Challenges; Digging into MORE

"There is always MORE, if you have the courage to dig deep enough."

Imagine a young girl around eight years old walking along a country road, kicking the dirt on the gravel road and thinking about life and all the wonderful adventures that await her. She is enjoying the moment with the hot summer sun beating down on her, but also understanding that there is more out there. Then imagine this same girl five years later navigating the complex halls of high school, weaving her way through a time of change. Fear, excitement and insecurity are all wrapped up in this very intense period of her life. This teen then becomes a young woman facing her fears and heading off to university to test her knowledge and open her world. Upon graduation she leaves the familiar comforts behind, heads off to the big city where love, marriage, children and professional growth follow through the years. The driving force for this woman is to dig in and get more deeply into her life. She stumbles often along the way, but starts to see a pattern. There are certain principles that emerge from this pattern that bring clarity and vision to her. Viewing this life one would see that it is not necessarily glamorous , but the truth of the story is that it is an exceptional life. This capacity for exceptional living is within anyone who truly wants it. I, in fact, was this girl and continue to be this woman walking along a path that has come to make sense to me. Using the principles I have developed over the years I hope to be able to help you decide if you truly want an exceptional life and, if you do, to show you how you can make it happen. MORE is at the heart of my philosophy of exceptional living. If you want to live an exceptional life, be prepared to deal with the challenges and difficulties that come with it. Through practicing this philosophy there is a path to living a life with true satisfaction and purpose.

MORE is an acronym for "Movement, Opportunity, Reality, and Exception."

M–Movement
O–Opportunity
R–Reality
E–Exception

The MORE philosophy is not about things, or the accumulation of wealth, or living life in pursuit of some elusive entity that fills up your life. Financial success is admirable, but it may not be wise to build your well-being entirely on wealth or accomplishments. Being attentive and present in each moment, while enjoying your life, may be ultimately more important. The MORE philosophy is quite the opposite of focusing exclusively on financial success; it is about getting a substantial experience out of your life. Living a unique and exceptional life is at the core of the MORE philosophy. Becoming increasingly present, additionally connected and authentically fulfilled is the goal.

Prior to really digging in, let's do a brief overview of the four words of this philosophy so that you can understand how they connect into a pattern and are at the core of everything else to come in this book. The illustration above shows how these four words converge in the moment. No matter what the situation is in front of you, these four principles can be applied to create a response on how to deal with that moment. It is a simple structure that can assist you in any circumstance and bring clarity to the choices and actions required of you in that moment.

The first letter of MORE is "M" and it stands for "Movement"

Life is moving forward whether we like it or not. It is my hope that this book will encourage movement in the reader. To feel stuck is incredibly frustrating, and wastes considerable energy. You may have some stuck spots in your life and "M" represents the action that is required to get things moving. There is no progression in an action plan without movement. "Movement" is "action."

The second letter in MORE is "O" and it stands for "Opportunity"

Take the opportunities that are in front of you, and recognize that even the most difficult times are an opportunity for growth. Focusing on opportunity enables us to assess what is right in front of us, giving us the vision to reframe the moment as an opportunity for something valuable in our lives. It is also the ability to seize the moment. Once we understand this assessment skill, we have the ability to deal with and utilize all the aspects of our lives. "Opportunity" is "assessment."

The "R" in MORE is for "Reality"

We need to have honest conversations with ourselves in order to get the most out of the life we have been given. When we can see the reality, we get the true information we need to make decisions. We need to pay attention to the "reality checks" that life offers. "Reality" is "information."

The "E" in MORE is for "Exception"

It is for daring to be the unique exception that you are and thus living an exceptional life. Each of us is one of a kind, and when we take the risk to be true to ourselves, we bring our best to the world and achieve a heightened experience of the world. This is the goal we are aiming for when we examine the steps to exceptional living. "Exception" is the "outcome."

The MORE philosophy is at the heart of this book and at the heart of my life. These four elements can inform any moment we encounter and assist us in how to respond to our lives.

M–Movement = action
O–Opportunity = assessment
R–Reality = information
E–Exception = outcome

The First Principle is Movement
"You have to move it, move it!"

The first principle of MORE is "Movement." Without movement, life is stagnant. We feel alive and vital as long as things are moving. When things get "plugged up" there is pressure. Life is like a garden hose: if there is an obstruction or knot in the hose, the water cannot pass through and the pressure builds to the point that it eventually bursts. There needs to be flow and movement. In comparison, think about a pool of water without movement; in essence, it becomes contaminated and even dangerous. Water is the essence of life and essential to humans, but water that is stagnant for a long period of time can become filled with bacteria that are harmful to us.

This principle is the same for us, emotionally and psychologically, as well as physically. Water that has movement is vibrant, refreshing, and brings us life. We use it to nourish and cleanse

4

our bodies, as well as to play and celebrate. Intrinsically, humans are drawn to the movement of water in rivers, lakes, and oceans. Every summer we find ourselves packing our picnic and toys, and heading out to the nearest body of water. Our bodies, our spirits, and our minds are not meant to be sedentary, without movement. When we experience movement in our lives, we celebrate and feel refreshed and invigorated. In every aspect of our human experience, we are built for movement. Therefore, if we do not provide movement for our minds, we create problems. We either shut down or we spin around on the same old information.

Jason

To understand the importance of movement, let's take a look at Jason. Everything about Jason indicates his life should be exceptional. He did very well in high school, is tall and handsome, his parents are wealthy, people find him charming, and he was always told he had so much potential. This young man is now twenty four and undoubtedly highly intelligent, but he is still living in his parents' basement. He is also unable to find a job or a school program that will hold his interest. Why is this happening?

Through the years he was told how smart he was, but he has always feared that he could not live up to those expectations. He does not feel he deserved the marks he got in high school as he never really tried, and he has now failed several of his post-secondary courses, as he did not attend class or even open the textbook. He finds himself frustrated with the smallest of things, including his parents' endless promptings to do something with his life. In essence, he is spending less and less time with friends and family, as he does not want to explain why his life looks the same or worse than it did five years ago. Instead, he prefers to spend most of his time on his computer, and feels that his virtual world is much more interesting than the real world. This is happening because there is no movement in his life and Jason is stuck!

When we think about Jason living in his parents' basement without any progression in his life, we know he is getting depressed and disconnected. His thoughts are increasingly negative and he is critical of himself and others. He has taken himself out of "the game" and does not want to participate, but his thoughts are increasingly toxic to him. The mind, just like the body, must move; without direction, the mind begins to twirl and swirl over the same things, particularly if we do not provide it with new information and stimulation. This is where the bacteria of the mind can begin to develop.

Jason needs to get some movement happening in his life in order to live an exceptional life. As stated before, thoughts and feelings without movement can become toxic, limiting us and keep us away from what we need. Consequently, movement is essential to our life and health. There is no exceptional living without movement.

The Second Principle is Opportunity
"When opportunity knocks…"

The second principle of MORE is "Opportunity." Life is filled with opportunity. It is a series of different opportunities with a series of different possible outcomes. It is not possible to take every opportunity, but if we take no risks, constantly hesitate, and let all the opportunities pass by, our lives will become stagnant and have no movement. Time keeps moving regardless of what we do. So as time moves, windows of opportunity will come and go, some of which we will take and some we will not. We can be creative forces in our own lives by choosing which windows of opportunity we will open and move through. Not every opportunity has assured success nor can we expect a great outcome from every choice. Each opportunity can be a learning experience if we allow it and open ourselves up to see what lesson lies within.

The best guides to choosing your opportunities are your

curiosity and your fear. Stay curious in life and you will have some interesting experiences. However, if you find yourself fearing the opportunity be warned that it just might be the one you need to pursue. There is an amazing liberation in transforming a fear by taking it on as an opportunity and moving through it. This is how we build our confidence, competence and sense of courage and self in the world. In the end, courage is the reward that comes from working through a fear. Furthermore, it is important to understand that opportunities seldom come when we are ready.

When I really look at each big change, turning point, or accomplishment in my life, I do not believe I was ready for any one of them. An opportunity usually comes before we are ready, so you cannot wait for the right time to take it. Instead, you can choose to take an opportunity when it is presented to you, "ready or not"! It is very important to understand that mistakes and difficult situations are the "yellow brick roads" of opportunities. They are life's way of teaching us lessons and leading us forward into growth and movement.

Brianne

To illustrate how ignoring or disguising mistakes can lead to missed opportunities let's look at Brianne. She is in her third year of university, taking a degree in chemical engineering, but feeling increasingly paralyzed by anxiety and seldom enjoying her life. In the past, she was always successful with friends, academics, and sports. She received a scholarship at the university she applied to, and travelled to the other side of the country to attend this prestigious school. Everyone told her how she was so lucky to be accepted at this school and to receive a scholarship.

It would look as if Brianne was taking every opportunity. The opposite is true. Brianne is actually missing the opportunities right in front of her. Although everything looks like it is happening for her, in reality she has not told anybody how difficult things have really been for her since she left home to come to school. She hates making mistakes and is at risk of failing some of her classes for the first time in her life. Overall, she is not getting the same high marks she did last year, and she feels herself slipping deeper into a hole.

In addition, she is struggling with how she can keep pretending that everything is okay, when everything seems to be at risk of falling apart. She does not want her parents to know what is happening as they might be disappointed in her. Her fear is that she is a big fake and that she doesn't have it all together the way everyone thinks she does. She increasingly fantasizes about disappearing, or just crawling into her bed and not coming out of her room for months. In addition, she is beginning to feels increased anxiety and avoids the classes she is struggling with and, although knowing that this is the wrong thing to do, she just feels too overwhelmed to attend. Not even her best friends know what she is going through. Inevitably, she feels alone and like a failure.

Brianne was fighting against these lessons and learning opportunities and trying to cover up her mistakes by telling her parents and friends that everything was great at school. Consequently, she did not want to reveal her struggles, and her desire to be perfect and have it all together is actually keeping her stuck. She was not taking the biggest opportunity that was in front of her; increasingly, she was hiding from it. If we are real with ourselves and approach a mistake or a difficult situation in an open non-defensive manner we can find the nugget that will assist us in growing and moving toward something exceptional. It is through our challenges and mistakes that we develop resilience and adaptability.

Our strength and health emerge after we have revealed a mistake or worked through something difficult and humbling. There is no doubt this is difficult, as our instinct is to run and cover up these things. If Brianne could begin to see the learning opportunity in her mistakes and reveal her struggles, she could get the assistance she needs and learn more about who she really is in this world. Her energy has been spent trying to keep up the façade of having everything together, and she is reaching the point of exhaustion. The path to a more authentic and fulfilled life is there for Brianne, but she has not been able to accept her mistakes as opportunities yet. The courage it takes to face the fear, and the humbling that is needed to take responsibility for a mistake, is an essential key to using opportunities as stepping stones to achieving a more balanced life.

The Third Principle is Reality
"Time for a Reality Check"

Hand in hand with principle two is the concept of reality. To achieve the outcome of an exceptional life you need to live in the real world! Living in a fantasy will only yield a fantasy, and frankly that is pretty unfulfilling. A fantasy may be pretty and perfect and have a "happy" ending, but it is not real. It is insubstantial and nothing else truly exists there but your imagination. It is healthy to have fantasies, to use your imagination to create visions for the future, but those exceptional moments that offer opportunity and require movement, only exist in the real world.

Fantasy, imagination, and visionary thinking are essential, but in order for vision to have an impact, there needs to be an action that then emerges in the real world. This information is the R of the MORE philosophy. We need to recognize fantasy and wishes for what they are, and pay attention to the real world that is right in front of us. It is filled with people, noise, smells, and sounds, and although amazingly beautiful it is messy and ugly at times.

Life is meant to have all the elements. There is no relationship of substance without some disappointments and difficulties. Without despair there is no joy. Without tears there is no laughter. There is a duality to the real world and therefore, the entire picture helps us appreciate and enjoy what is in front of us. If every day were Christmas, it might feel great for a few days, but then this "special" occasion would become old and "not so special." Life is meant to change and have room for both the special and the mundane.

Life provides "reality checks," and we need to pay attention to them. Often we do not want to see the reality check, because we have attached ourselves to a fantasy or a hope for the future that will not allow us to accept the reality of today.

Susie

Susie is thirty five and wanted nothing more than to be a Mom, to live in a loving home, and be the best wife and mother possible. She knows that her husband Randy treats her poorly, and never seems to appreciate all the things she does for him and their daughter. He was never faithful to her, even when they were dating, but he told her that he would change when he became a father. She feels stuck, but does not really want to change things. She tells herself that the right thing to do is to stay with Randy as she wants her daughter to grow up with both her parents, and not live in a broken home. Randy has always wanted a son, and Susie sometimes wonders whether, if they had another child, this would change things and bring their family closer. On some level, though, she knows this is not the answer. Their home is not a healthy, happy place for her daughter, but Susie talks herself into staying, because she keeps the hope alive that one day it might get better. Susie has attached herself to her wishes for her life and is ignoring the reality of her life. Without paying attention to the reality, she will continue to miss opportunities for movement and growth, and she will stay stuck and unhappy.

Just like Susie, we have all used one form of justification or another, but the whole time, if we listen and pay attention, our intuition is trying to give us a reality check. Oddly, it is our intuition that is trying to tell us the truth, the real story, and it is our mind that is telling us the make-believe story.

Reality checks are often painful and difficult, but if you do not heed them, they tend to come back harder, more strongly, and more painfully. In the end, the cost of denying reality becomes very high indeed. If you fight it, the reality check costs you more as time passes. If you listen and accept the reality check, it will lead you toward the exceptional life you seek. The gift is that it is never too late to listen to the reality check and turn things around, but the work will be harder the longer you wait.

Intrinsically, the longer Susie ignores what is going on in her life, the more difficult it will be to turn it around. If she continues on as she is, she will increasingly disconnect from her intuition and her purpose. We limit our ability to participate and contribute if we are stepping out of the real world. What we have to contribute always means the most when we are being real. Our reality checks can lead us toward purpose. There is a great stimulation and rush in being authentic and offering the world what you really have.

The Fourth Principle is Exception
"Dare To Be Different"

Let's now take a look at the final principle of MORE, and the meaning of the word "exceptional."

The "E" of MORE stands for the daring to be the exception, and to live the exceptional life. In order to understand this concept, we need to define what "being exceptional" actually means, and then decide if an exceptional life is the life you truly want. According to the Merriam-Webster Dictionary, "exceptional" means:

1. Forming an exception: rare.
2. Better than average: superior.
3. Deviating from the norm.

So, an exceptional life is one in which we are aiming higher than the average and is a move away from the ordinary into the extraordinary.

When they hear the word "exceptional," many people think it means "great" or "terrific," but in fact it means something quite different. Something or someone who is exceptional often stands alone or apart. This is not an easy place to be, as we crave company and it is human nature to want to belong to the group. Although we may not mind standing out, we do not want to be lonely, and there are times when living an exceptional life means facing the fear of loneliness. The exceptional life is not the norm. Instead, it is the exception. The exceptional principle of MORE encourages you to take risks and to be the unique person you are. Overall, let your life flow with movement, embrace opportunities, and learn from them.

Christie

Christie is twenty-nine and running a successful software company. She is without a doubt "quirky," and has managed to take her quirks and turn them into a successful way of life.

When I first met Christie, she was fifteen and struggling in high school. She had never really fit in with the other students, and high school was a challenge as she felt alone and different from her peers. She did not have many friends and felt like an outsider. She was too tall, too intense, too loud, and too unusual for most of the people she went to school with. She did not care about fashion and did not want to talk about boys with all the other girls in her class. She loved to read, was designing her own websites, and felt a passion for cake decorating and animal rescue. There was nothing "cool" about Christie to her peers, but her warmth and passion are what really make Christie interesting.

There is no doubt that she was the exception among her peers. She worried about world issues like hunger and war, and struggled with some anxiety around these things. There were times she felt a lot of pain, and at times it was a struggle to be compassionate and caring without getting depressed by the pain in the world. She cared about people deeply and helped start a gay and lesbian support group at her school, even though she was not a lesbian herself. She also started an animal rights group and volunteered at a community kitchen to serve meals to those in need.

She was definitely not the norm, and she suffered at times, as she still wanted to belong. But she grew to understand that she had a lot to contribute and her position as an outsider helped her understand and assist marginalized groups. She found a great sense of purpose in her social activism, and as she used her courage to help others she also grew more and more confident in her unique self.

At twenty-four she graduated from university and joined a large electronic media company where she soon moved to the top. Then when she was twenty-seven, she left that position and started her own company with her husband who was a computer programmer. Their company is doing very well and both of them are very excited to be living exceptional lives in which their unique talents are utilized consistently. Christie and her husband are not afraid to be different and unique. They are both committed to assisting others, and part of their profit each year goes toward a foundation they have started that builds schools around the world.

These are exceptional people, living exceptional lives, and doing exceptional things. Once Christie understood that she could be the exception and did not have to fit in, she found her true self and felt great joy in creating and contributing.

The Origins of the Philosophy behind MORE

I also recall struggling to fit in when I was young. When I look back, I realize that is when my understanding of the principle of exception emerged. I have certainly noticed the times when I did not feel that I belonged as my life progressed. I was a thoughtful child who felt as though I were different, but I also wanted to be a part of something bigger. I paid close attention to what was going on around me and I was always curious about people and life. Like any child, I experienced great joys and heartbreaks.

My first few years of life were on a farm and then we moved to a small Saskatchewan town in Canada's Prairies. It was not an idyllic childhood, but it was a great childhood filled with many fond memories. My parents did not have a lot of money and they worked hard for everything they got. They always provided for me and my brother, but nobody grew up entitled in my family. My brother is two and half years older than me and even then, he was one of my favourite playmates. Our parents both worked and we children were expected to pitch in around the house as well as manage our independence.

Hard work was not an option: it was just a way of life. I do not remember resenting the work that was expected of me; rather it made me feel significant and an important member of the family. My parents were busy working at their jobs or working around the house and yard, but we still had time for fun when the work was done. We did our chores and still had the time and independence to wander through town visiting friends, making up creative games to play, and exploring the area. I enjoyed those explorations with my brother; they included moments of long silences as well as great conversations. Sometimes we would discuss the minutiae of life and sometimes we would discuss the meaning of life and our hopes for the future. Yes, there was a freedom of movement and what now seems like an abundance of time.

It was on one of these walks when I had the first stirrings of thoughts behind what eventually became my philosophy of MORE. I just knew in my heart that this life was an incredible journey and I felt that there was something special out there for me. I wondered at the possibilities ahead and how I would experience this world and this life, and I wanted to do it in a way that would give me the most out of this experience. I did want an exceptional life; I just did not fully understand what I was seeking at that time. I wanted to be a part of something that mattered and I wanted to go deep into this life. I also understood that there was something very special right there in that simple moment of exploring the prairie countryside with my brother. I was a satisfied child but the thought of discovering new things in my life made me excited and curious. I feel very fortunate that I still enjoy conversations with my brother, as well as silences, and, occasionally bouncing a philosophical idea or two off him. I still feel the excitement of that young girl in me who is curious about the world; I continue to believe that we can all achieve a feeling of significance and joy in our lives.

Do You Have MORE in You?

Most people feel the possibilities that lie within, but for many of us, these possibilities feel out of reach or remain just around the corner. How do you achieve this exceptional life you seek? What does MORE really mean?

The meaning of the MORE philosophy is intertwined among its principles. As mentioned above, there are four principles that can be applied to life and any situation encountered along the way. In essence, MORE is a way of living life in which movement and growth emerge from paying attention to the opportunities and reality checks along the way, and having the courage to be the exception. MORE is the avenue to exceptional living that lies within each moment and within every one of us.

The next chapters will explain the MORE philosophy further and weave it into real-life examples and stories. At the end of each chapter, there will be some questions for you to think about and apply to your own life. These questions are there to assist you in applying the information from the book and giving the MORE philosophy a context in your own life. I encourage you to think about what you read, ask yourself the questions, talk with others if you want, jot down notes in a journal, and give it all some thought.

To get you started here are a few questions to help you begin your journey through the MORE philosophy.

Questions for Contemplation

Have you ever had that feeling that there was something special out there for you that you could not quite grasp yet?

When you take an action in life, how do you feel?

What happens to your mind and your body when you feel stuck on something?

Do you take the moment to assess the opportunity right in front of you?

When you make a mistake, do you try to hide it, defend it, forget about it, or analyze it?

Do you feel that you are able to be honest with yourself?

Are you aware of the reality checks in your life, or do you prefer to focus on the way you wish things to be?

Do you fear being alone?

Do you fear being lonely?

How do you feel when you have accomplished something you are proud of?

Do you fear standing up for something and being seen as unique, or does that excite you, or both?

CHAPTER TWO

Recognizing the Characteristics and Substance of an Exceptional Life; Allowing MORE.

"In allowing, MORE always happens."

It seems as though we are a culture searching for more in this life. We might not have the concrete struggles that previous generations experienced, but we certainly do have our own struggles; in essence, they are of a different kind. When I look around I see so many people trying to fill their lives with more stuff, more people, more rewards, and more indulgences. But there is something to this culture that seems unable to fill itself up. We remain hungry. We have become a society of consumers, spenders, and collectors of material things, measuring ourselves on this accumulation, but realizing that there is something that we are still looking for and craving. We want to feel full, but so many of us cannot recognize that full feeling when we have it, so we are trying to fill up on the wrong things.

In this chapter, I would like to share the stories of two people who look as though they should have it all, but they are both struggling. Each of these people has something in common with the other; they want to figure out why they are not satisfied when they have realized so many of their goals. There is something in their lives that does not feel quite right and they are not allowing themselves to truly be in their exceptional lives. In fact, they have the ingredients to live exceptional lives, but they are not sure how to get there. They are still looking for something in their lives, but they are looking in the wrong direction. They want an exceptional life, but they are finding themselves feeling more disconnected, lonelier, depleted and increasingly unfulfilled. Ultimately, this search for meaning and purpose can hit us in small ways or impact our lives at the core.

Bill

Bill, for example, is a successful business man in his mid-forties with his own business, an attractive wife, and two attractive children who go to private school, and yet, he still feels dissatisfied. Bill is actually in crisis although his life looks great from the outside. He has a big house, great clothes, and travels on luxury holidays at least twice a year. But Bill is feeling lost in his own life. He loves his family, but has trouble feeling engaged when he is with them.

When they go on holidays they stay in fancy resorts and do all the great activities one is supposed to do on these types of trips, yet Bill sometimes feels as if he is watching his children on a screen and he is separated from them. He says the things he is supposed to say, but his own voice does not sound real to him. He wonders if his family really knows him at all and if he knows them. He loves his wife and finds her attractive, but he feels that somehow he is a disappointment to her and he knows that she does not understand why he withdraws from her when she reaches out to him. He knows he has hurt her feelings and he feels guilty much of the time.

He travels a lot for work and misses his family when he is away, but when he is with them, he finds himself feeling irritated with the kids and unable to really connect with his wife. He cannot figure out his dissatisfaction, since he has everything he thought he wanted.

As his business has grown in success he has bought bigger houses, faster cars, and filled his life with all the amenities and luxuries. He finds himself increasingly questioning if he made the right choices, wondering what a different life might be like, and he is scared that he is more at ease when he is away from his family than when he is with them.

This was not the way he wanted his life to be. Bill is at risk to leave his family, although he loves and values them. He is so disconnected from himself that he just cannot effectively connect with those around him, and although he has been trying to fill his life with more stuff, he is missing the opportunities to make real movement in his life.

Bill is certainly not the only one struggling with a feeling of disconnection in his life. We need to only have a quick look at those around us to see that many people are experiencing lives that look successful from the outside, but they are not feeling satisfied on the inside. We may think that they have every reason to be happy, but what looks as if it should be happiness is not always so. There are many people wondering about why they do not feel happier in this life, and most of us have struggled at some point with feeling disconnected from our own lives and not being able to enjoy the good things that are happening right now.

This is a human struggle, and the MORE philosophy can assist each and every one of us with finding increased satisfaction and substance in our lives.

Trudy

Thirty-six-year-old Trudy is a registered nurse who has risen to Head Nurse on her unit. She feels accomplished in her work, but she just cannot seem to maintain a romantic relationship. She is smart, athletic, and commonly described as attractive.

Trudy is best friends with Susie that we met in the last chapter. They have known each other for many years and Trudy has watched Susie become increasingly unhappy in her marriage. Trudy has been the one Susie has turned to for support and Trudy has been a "rock" for Susie as she struggles in her marriage. Trudy is increasingly disillusioned and her biggest fear is always at the back of her mind—she fears being alone in life and that she will never find Mr. Right.

She has been in several relationships through the years, and been on dates recently, but there is always something wrong with the man or the situation. Her friends tell Trudy that she is too picky to have a real long-term relationship. Every man she dates is too tall, too short, too poor, or boring. Her latest date talked too much, and the date before that did not talk enough. The man her sister set her up with is nothing like whom she imagined herself being with. The one she met through online dating, she actually found attractive, but he was not somebody she would want fathering her children, and ultimately, she cannot imagine herself building a life with any of the men she has met. Her hopes of marriage and children seem to be disappearing.

She has always been outgoing and friendly, but finds that she is beginning to feel bitter around her friends. Many of them seem to have it all and she is scared that she will not get what they have. Then there are the friends like Susie who are stuck in unhealthy relationships and they present an even worse scenario to Trudy. She is beginning to think that there is nobody out there for her. When asked to join friends for a social event on her days off, she is increasingly saying no, preferring to just stay at home and retreat into her dreams of the perfect man, perfect children, and perfect home. It seems easier to isolate herself, than to keep trying.

Susie and Trudy work together at the hospital and did their nursing training together several years ago. Trudy has primarily concentrated on her career, while Susie works part time trying to balance her role as mother, wife, and nurse. Susie is sad most of the time and Trudy worries that Susie is getting depressed. Susie's husband Randy has already had a couple of affairs and is disrespectful to Susie, as he is always flirting with other women in front of Susie. Trudy does not understand why Susie keeps forgiving him and taking him back.

In turn, Trudy is determined that nothing like this will ever happen to her. The relationship choices out there seem dismal, as it seems that the good ones are gone and the others just do not interest her. As a result, she commits herself more and more to her career and plans on how she can accomplish the next move up the ladder at the hospital. Trudy always wanted to achieve a life where she could have it all, but she is now finding herself feeling stuck and scared. She keeps doing the things she is familiar with and hopes that they will distract her from her increasing fear that her life will not be exceptional at all.

But there are always ways to make movement in our lives, and there are many steps that Trudy can take that will lead her to an exceptional life.

Both Bill and Trudy are stuck, but the way out of these stuck places is to allow movement, opportunity, and reality to lead them to the exceptional lives they seek. Rather than fight against their lives, they need to learn to allow life to lead them forward, and in allowing this things start to happen. If they could open up to the opportunity in the moment, accept that an exceptional life may not look the way they had anticipated it would look, then they could each begin to transform the challenges and disappointments into movement.

An exceptional life will always have challenge in it. Reality is not always pretty, but it is attainable and not a fantasy. Each person's exceptional life is unique to that person. In essence, it does not have to look like anybody else's life. An exceptional life is forgiving, as it has the dignity and grace to allow each of us to make mistakes. These mistakes are essential to moving forward. As well, an exceptional life is interesting, engaging, satisfying, stimulating, as well as frustrating, disappointing, and aggravating.

As Bill begins to be honest with himself about his struggles rather than detach himself, he will get more engaged in his relationships and his life. His focus was always ahead of him and when he achieved his goals, he was surprised that he did not feel more joy. He forgot that joy occurs right in the moment, and is not something to be shelved for the future. As he allows joy and pain in his life, he will begin to see the opportunity to build deeper relationships with those he loves, but he needs to be honest about his fears in order to make movement. This is the MORE philosophy in action. As he gains comfort with allowing himself to feel more emotion, he will become more at ease with the emotions around him.

Trudy will need to take a real look at her expectations and the subsequent disappointments that these expectations have brought into her life. She will need to be honest about her growing bitterness so that she can move it toward acceptance. This presents an opportunity for her to let go of the feeling that she has to somehow control her life, and once she is honest and real with herself she can begin to allow the opportunities in the moments that are right in front of her. In allowing and letting go of control, things begin to happen. She might need to grieve some of the things she had hoped for at this point in her life in order to allow and accept the life that she has right now.

By using the MORE philosophy, both Bill and Trudy can begin to live truly authentic and exceptional lives, as they allow the pain and joy that occurs while on a journey of a lifetime.

Questions for Contemplation

Do you feel stuck in any area of your life?

Are you aware of any patterns that are getting in the way?

Do you feel as if you are caught in a pattern that you are having trouble getting out of?

Can you remember moments that you felt detached from your own life?

What are your expectations for your life?

Have you met those expectations?

Do you feel you need to control your life?

What are the disappointments in your life?

Do you struggle with letting go and allowing life to lead you?

Do you believe that things work out as they need to in the end?

What is your greatest desire?

What is your greatest fear?

Think of one risk/opportunity you took.

How did it play out?

Are you able to hear feedback about yourself from others?

Do you want an exceptional life?

CHAPTER THREE

Creating an Exceptional Life; Shifting From Idealistic to Realistic; Rising to the Call for Action.

"I cannot be perfect and fabulous, so I choose fabulous."

How do we live an exceptional life, and what are the actual steps to get there? Where and how do we begin to make practical movement and start to experience the wonder of this life?

Since "Movement" is the first principle of the MORE philosophy, it follows that this book will outline a step-by-step action plan that creates an exceptional life. Since it is designed, not only as an introduction to the MORE philosophy but also as a practical guide book, I view the steps I present throughout the book as points of interest along a nature walk. Along any well-built nature trail, there are points of interest that can be used and viewed at any time, and a series of arrows that remind us to keep going in the right direction so that we do not get too distracted, or even worse, lost. It is helpful to have these practical pointers that keep us moving and help us orient ourselves as we go.

Life is not a straight and stagnant journey, but rather a series of steps on a path that has some unexpected turns. Just like life, that nature trail has purpose: it is heading somewhere beautiful and interesting although we are not sure what is around the corner. The path is there to keep us oriented and moving in the right direction. But, no matter how beautiful the forest, if we get lost without a path, it will be a very difficult journey. We may be so busy trying to find our way while attempting to survive, that we forget to see the beauty around us.

Life is much like those nature trails, and this book is the guide that will keep you moving as well as remind you to pay attention to what you see along the way.

I present here the sixteen steps that comprise the optimal way to keep moving along our life path. These are the reminders and pointers that make for an exceptional journey. The rest of this book expands on these steps.

The 16 Steps to Living an Exceptional Life

1. Turn it Up to Eleven.
2. Give Up Perfectionism and Become An Exceptionalist.
3. Get your Ass in the Right Spot.
4. Accept the Human Moments.
5. Quiet the Chatter.
6. Accept the Good with the Bad.
7. Learn from your Mistakes.
8. Stop Making Excuses.
9. When Things get Tough, Remember "I Can Handle it."
10. Learn How to Wield Your Double-Edged Sword.
11. Contribute to Others.
12. Know Which Side of Yourself to Pull on at the Right Time.
13. Stay Curious.
14. Accept that You Too Will Die.
15. Give Up Idealism and Become a Realistic Optimist.
16. Move Purpose and Passion in the Same Direction.

Step #1: Turn it Up to Eleven

To obtain our exceptional life, we need to be willing to push the boundaries past simple comfort and take risks.

It brings to mind a movie I saw years ago called This is Spinal Tap. In this rockumentary by Rob Reiner, the filmmaker was interviewing the guitar player of a fictionalized, hard rock band.

The oblivious lead guitar player had the number eleven on his guitar amp, and the interviewer asked him why he had an amplifier that went to eleven when the loudest sound the amplifier was able to make was already set to the number ten. The character paused, looked perplexed, and then replied, "But it goes to eleven!" I have always loved that remark, and it was one of my favourite moments in the movie.

In many ways, an exceptional life is a life that stretches a little farther and pumps up the volume just a little louder. An exceptional life is about your own internal experience rather than an external motivation. If you want your life to go to eleven, even when everyone tells you it should only go to ten, ignore those preconceptions and take it to eleven.

As in the "E" Principle of the MORE philosophy, dare to be different and do it your way. You do not have to follow all the rules and conceptions that have been set out for you. Learn the rules as you go, but do not be afraid to challenge them as well. It is not only okay, but essential, to bring your own flair to a situation.

This is not a book about how to have a happy life. Rather this is a book about how to have an exceptional life. A life that goes to eleven! Joy is a part of that life, but like every other emotion, this will come and go; life is not meant to stagnate. There is no achieved state of higher consciousness that is called happiness that remains joyful and peaceful at all times. Every feeling will come and go. Even though the external volume is the same at ten as it is at eleven, there is something accomplished when we abandon those external ideas of the volume of our success and focus on creating an eleven within. This lets us see how far we can push ourselves and enhance our own life experience. This eleven is our very own unique contribution and the special spark that is you, and only you.

When I refer to taking life to eleven, I do not mean trying to achieve the unachievable, but rather bringing your best self to the plate and be willing to take risks. I also mean abandoning yourself to the experience in order to get the most out of it. In essence, be playful, take a risk, and allow yourself to feel the eleven in ten sometimes. You are in control of the volume and there is nothing really stopping you from experiencing an eleven inside, when you want to.

Step #2: Give Up Perfectionism and Become An Exceptionalist

Why is it essential to let go of perfectionism? Because it is getting in your way, and if you take a perfectionistic path, you will never accomplish an exceptional life. The two cannot exist together. Perfectionism is the arch enemy. Perfectionism can never be accomplished, as perfect does not exist. Perfectionism is the antithesis of the MORE philosophy, as there is no reality in it.

An exceptional life is a choice we make. It is important to understand that an exceptional life has nothing to do with perfection or perfecting your life. An exceptional life can be highly imperfect. In fact, it must be imperfect. We have to choose to be imperfect and allow the learning that imperfection brings.

To help illustrate the mind shift from perfectionism to exceptionalism, I am going to share my own "aha!" moment on this topic. On occasion, I have been accused of being a perfectionist, but it never felt right when people called me that. Even though I have always wanted to accomplish things of substance, and have put a lot of energy and thought into the things I have undertaken, the word "perfectionism" just did not feel right. Still, I sometimes thought of myself as a frustrated perfectionist, as I knew that perfectionism could only lead to frustration and it was a setup for failure, but I was also driven to do my best. A half job never felt acceptable to me. I just did not know a better word than "perfectionism" to describe my approach to life, but I always knew there had to be another way of looking at the drive to accomplish and succeed without putting it in a perfectionistic frame.

How could we accomplish something perfect? The word alone indicated that I would not be able to accomplish it. How could I reach perfection?

When I was younger I might have had perfectionist tendencies. I wanted approval and wanted to be accepted and liked by others. I wanted acknowledgement for doing things very well, but in my mind I always fell short of the ideal. I think this is an experience that most of us can relate to, as it is natural to want approval. We want to matter to those who matter to us. This desire to be of significance can lead us to trying to be perfect in order to get attention and approval. But being "perfect" will always feel outside your grasp, like reaching for something at the back of the cupboard that you know is there but you just can't quite touch. The frustration of not reaching the desired object leaves you feeling inadequate and dissatisfied.

I have seen the cost of perfectionism and how it actually diminishes our human potential. I have seen people rendered immobile in life by their desire for perfection, giving up on their goals because they did not feel they could accomplish what they wanted. I have seen many people opting out before even starting the race. I have seen people not take risks or pursue goals out of the fear of the judgement of others, as well as their own self-judgement. It has always struck me as such a loss when somebody gives up before really trying. It is such a waste of vision when people set their expectations so high that they can never bring their goal into reality and they do not even dare to try. For those who do pursue perfectionism, it is a waste of energy as they will never accomplish that goal.

If we allow ourselves to get lost in perfectionistic tendencies, and to either give into the relentless drive to achieve the unachievable or to opt out due to fear, then we will limit our creativity and our ability to impact others. In order to allow our potential to flourish, we need to develop realistic goals without opting out. So, if perfectionism is destructive, but you are still a driven high-functioning person, then what term works best to describe your path to success?

The moment of clarity came to me through a friend who is also a therapist with a similar drive for success. We were discussing my latest idea and a bold move I was making in my career. As usual we both had a lot on the go and several goals we wanted to accomplish. We met for dinner and had a chance to catch up on each other's lives. She supportively listened to my ideas around the bold move I wanted to make professionally that had many risks involved.

I envisioned transforming a private psychology centre into an agent of change. I saw a vision where I could create an umbrella in which the therapist would be free to concentrate on bringing their best to the clients, and the clients would become familiar with a brand that they knew would bring them top quality service and practical information. Quintessentially, the practice I was working at had a good, long-standing reputation and the primary owner was retiring; I saw this as an opportunity to bring my visions to reality–an exceptional opportunity to impact my profession and the larger community.

I could see an infrastructure that handled the business aspects seamlessly for both the clients and the Associates. Meanwhile, we would create a team of top specialists who would push to grow professionally, as well as bring the MORE philosophy to the clients. I passionately wanted to change the way the general public perceived and understood counselling. I wanted to demonstrate that this service could be of concrete value to everyone who chose to use it. I wanted to break the stigma that is often associated with counselling by having honest conversations that brought psychology out of the ivory towers of academia, out of the hidden counselling rooms, and into the real world. I wanted therapists to be at the forefront of change and looking for ways to contribute to the community as well as to their clients.

There was nothing small about my vision and it would take considerable financial risk, time, and effort to transform the practice into the thriving vibrant centre of change and contribution that I envisioned.

After hearing my vision and the heights I was aiming for,

my trusted friend looked at me and said "Alyson, it is not that you are a perfectionist, it is just that you want everything to be exceptional."

The light bulb went on. I am not a perfectionist, but rather, I am an "exceptionalist": I can be the exception! This was an "aha!" moment for me! Why wouldn't I want to create the most exceptional practice possible? Why wouldn't we as humans want to create the most exceptional lives possible?

This was what I had always felt, even as that young girl wandering around the small prairie town walking and talking with my brother. As far as I know, this is the only life I have, and I want to have an exceptional experience while I am here. I also want to assist others in realizing this potential within themselves and creating their own exceptional experiences.

Life is a gift, but that gift sometimes comes in a package that we wish were different from the one we received. But we must accept the package we receive in order to have an exceptional life. Unlike the frustrating path of perfectionism, the exceptional life is achievable and real. It is based in reality, not on expectations and ideals that we can never reach.

Trudy, in the last chapter, would need to come to terms with her perfectionistic tendencies and her expectations in order to be present in the life she has. Real life gets messy, dirty, and complicated at times. Real exceptional lives require real exceptional risks as well.

If an exceptional life is your goal, then there should be no more reaching into the back of the cupboard to try to grab some unseen object that you can't grasp. If you want an exceptional life, you are going to have to let go of the excuses and be honest with yourself. An exceptional life will require some things of you, but it is not hidden at the back of a cupboard.

This is a life that is real and solid, that we can grasp and hold in our hands, and warm our hearts with. It is also a life that can terrify us, as an exceptional life is not necessarily an easy, tidy life. This is not a quest for average and the norm, this is a journey of exception. Some will celebrate the gift of their lives with us, as we share ours with others, but also be warned that others might feel overwhelmed and threatened by your exceptional life. Furthermore, this path is not a popularity contest and if you are constantly seeking approval, the path to an exceptional life will bring you face to face with your painful desire for acceptance by others.

Not every exceptional life is a larger-than-life experience, nor is every moment of an exceptional life filled with awe and wonder. We can sit quietly with it and feel excited and at peace at the same time. There may be quiet moments and loud moments, but the common theme is feeling alive and engaged in your own life. Sometimes we may want the volume on low; sometimes we want to turn it up to eleven. In order to do this we have to accept the life we have and know how we can use the power of choice as our volume control. We need to be aware of our strengths and vulnerabilities, and how to create the most exceptional experience with the material, circumstances, and creativity that we have within. The ability to lead an incredible and exceptional life is truly within each of us.

Questions for Contemplation

Do you consider yourself a perfectionist?

Do you set goals and accomplish them?

What gets in the way of your accomplishing a goal?

Do you procrastinate?

Are you concerned about how others perceive you?

Do you consider yourself an approval seeker?

If people criticize your idea or accomplishment, does it feel like they are criticizing you?

What does "being exceptional" mean to you?

Would you be willing to risk the approval of others for an idea you believe in?

Do you feel regret for opportunities that you did not take?

Are you at ease with being on your own, or do you prefer to be part of the group?

Are you an innovator? Do you like to be at the forefront of change?

Do you like to break the rules or follow them?

Do you feel that you are able to allow yourself to feel the eleven in a ten sometimes?

CHAPTER FOUR

Staying Present and in the Moment; Recognizing Retrograde Action; The Ass-Backward Theory.

"There is no way to say this delicately:
we are approaching the best things in life ass-backward."

So what is the Ass-Backward Theory? It is one of the greatest challenges and one of the greatest blocks to a truly exceptional life.

Basically, the premise is as follows: in our modern society we have turned intimacy upside down, and we often experience the most powerful moments of connection with another person "backwards." The moments that are meant to be intimate and savored are too overwhelming for people, so they detach when they need to be present. Conversely, the moments that are not meant to be personal are the ones that people attach themselves to. This is the reason that we can fixate on a situation that is not really important in the big picture, while not paying attention to the moment that is truly important.

Self-Protection Needs ~ The Alarm

Have you ever had a moment when somebody cut in front of you while driving and you were so outraged that it became the most dominant feeling you had, and it affected the rest of your day? Have you ever dwelt on this and started calling that person names in your head, or, even worse, verbally exploded on some stranger? Many otherwise rational people experience road rage, or road outrage, when somebody cuts in front of them in traffic. Yes, poor driving is a safety hazard, but the rage we can feel in these circumstances does not always make sense.

Most of us have found ourselves dwelling on incidents like these. When we perceive that somebody has been unfair or rude to us, we often create a story in our minds as to how disrespectful that person was and we then feel justified to carry our wronged feelings long past the situation.

Then, there are the moments when you are having a real connection with somebody and you draw back. You do not know why you are drawing back, but all of a sudden it feels like it is too much. You might even remember feeling this with the people you love the most.

Although many of us hope to find romantic love there are times when that person we are in love with is right in front of us looking deeply into our eyes and we are overwhelmed by the depth of the moment; we are unable to deal with our own overwhelm so we disconnect and quickly look away and change the topic. Why do we do this? Because we fear vulnerability.

When you truly connect and are present with another human being you create a powerful emotional vulnerability in yourself and others. Disconnection is a self-protective mechanism that is activated when we feel highly vulnerable. This self-protection then leads us to pull back and withdraw. We are not always aware that we are doing this, but rather we sometimes find ourselves feeling dissatisfied and confused when we know we should be feeling joyful and connected. It is a survival technique, but unfortunately it guards us from that which we most desire–a true connection with another human being.

When we recall from the second chapter Bill, who seemed to have it all, we remember that he was disconnecting from himself and his family as he was guarding against feeling vulnerable in the world.

Much too often we end up focusing on the wrong things,

while the things we really should focus on are quickly brushed by, politely acknowledged, or ignored altogether. It is easier to get upset about the things that do not deeply matter. Humans are programmed to self-protect. It is in our genetic make-up. We are products of our history, and humans have a long history that started with some real dangers.

Back in prehistoric times, when we were fighting the elements, and life was based on survival of the fittest, it did not pay to be vulnerable. This is the way the "cave man" part of our brain operates: through the fight-or-flight response. There is nothing wrong with this instinct, and in fact this survival instinct is what has helped humans survive and thrive through our existence on this planet. However, we are no longer fighting for survival in the way we once needed to. Modern reality is that very few humans in our Western world are truly threatened with losing their lives on a daily basis anymore. I am not saying that there are not real physical threats out there, and there is no doubt that some people experience truly significant dangers and suffer physical harm, but on the whole, most of us do not experience life threatening danger daily.

When humans had daily threats to their lives they needed to constantly protect against vulnerability in order to survive. Our brain became wired with an alarm to let us know when we were in danger. In that context, it makes sense that the better the alarm, the better the chances for survival. In our modern world we are not sure what to do with this alarm, and we either turn it into anxiety or disconnection.

Emotional Vulnerability ~ Fight or Flight

To illustrate how powerful our fear of vulnerability is, I will share the story of a moment of intense vulnerability from my own life.

When I became a mother, I remember thinking that I would never be able to feel secure in the world in the same way. To become a parent is a whole new level of vulnerability. I am the mother of twins, and their birth had some complications, as multiple births often do. My son stopped breathing within minutes of being born and after being revived was immediately taken to the neonatal intensive care unit. I was a new parent, and the new parent of two children at once, and it did not matter that I was a professional therapist and a parent educator. My newborn child was in danger and nothing had prepared me for the vulnerability I felt in those moments.

I remember the panic, the absolute overwhelm of that moment, and the desire to detach from it all. I wanted to know what was happening to him, but I also wanted the emotional pain and anxiety to just stop. I was still in the operating room when he was taken away, and I could not move. Part of me wanted to run down the hall to the neonatal unit, while another part just wanted to float away.

That desire to run down the hall was my fight instinct as I wanted to get into that neonatal room and do anything I could to help him. That desire to float away was my flight instinct and I wanted to retreat into self-protection.

I also remember in that instant having another "aha!" moment. I said to myself, "Alyson, you cannot have the big love without the big risk." I still believe this to be true. His life was out of my hands, and I was dependent on the skills of others as well as on a bit of luck. Fortunately, he received excellent care and made it through this crisis, but this incident led me deeper into understanding the ass-backward theory, as well as examining my relationship with vulnerability.

Hey, you stole my spot!

What does this have to do with the ass-backward theory? Well, quite a lot actually.

Since we do not have daily physical dangers to contend with, we use our self-protective instincts to protect ourselves against emotional vulnerability. Our caveman brain thinks it is safe when it focuses on the things that do not make us feel vulnerable; thus, the intense focus on the things that are not that important like having a parking stall taken by another. Those are the moments that the "ass" of the ass-backward theory is in charge.

To have an exceptional life, one will have to recognize those moments when we are putting too much emphasis on the wrong thing. In essence this is putting our ass in the wrong spot. Do you really want the focus of your day to be somebody stealing your parking spot, or would you rather keep things moving by recognizing the feeling of frustration, feeling the emotion, and then letting it go? The choice is yours. You can free yourself from this very quickly by allowing the feeling, but then moving the feeling.

This is the "M" in the MORE philosophy again. Just keep that water flowing through the garden hose and the pressure will not build up. If we make a big deal of it and dwell on the feeling we are creating unnecessary pressure.

Try taking the focus off the person who annoyed you and focus on something that brings back the joyful feeling. Is the sun shining? Are you looking forward to seeing your family when you get home? Did it feel great when you grabbed the shopping cart and somebody had left the quarter in it so you didn't need to dig around your pocket to find change? Look to the things that refocus you, so that you do not dwell on something that just wastes your time and does not bring anything of value into your life.

In those moments when you allow the "ass" to be in charge, try to think of something you are grateful for and gratitude will always get you back in alignment. Who does deserve your focus in your life? It probably is not the person who stole the parking spot. If we focus on those unimportant moments we might be creating an unexceptional life.

Step #3 ~ Get Your Ass in the Right Spot

All love, attachment, and connection have some risk. The reason we turn things backwards is because of our emotional vulnerability. But it is a faulty protection, as it does not truly protect us from getting hurt.

To be honest with ourselves, we must acknowledge that hurt is not a possibility in a significant relationship; it is inevitable. If we accept and have an awareness of this, we may be able to turn the "ass-backward" forward again. We may be able to put the ass where it really belongs, rather than have the ass in charge. We all know that it is not a good thing to have an ass in charge of any project, let alone the really important projects. We all need our ass and when the ass is in its right spot it does well, but it really needs to know its place and stay there.

In order to live an exceptional life, we will need to recognize our desire to detach, and at times we will need to fight to keep ourselves present in those relationships in which we will be hurt. If our ass is in the right place, our heart can better experience our moments of love and connection. We need to stop wasting our time focusing on the unimportant things just because if feels safer for us, and accept that those powerful, important moments might have some fear and sadness attached to them. In significant relationships there is always potential for pain, and this leads to love and loss becoming tangled up together.

Bobby and Joseph

This simple story illustrates how love and loss exist together. Bobby was playing ball in the backyard with his father Joseph. Bobby started throwing the ball at the house and his father told him to slow down before his ball ended up on the roof.

Of course, now that this idea had been introduced five-year-old Bobby rose to the challenge and threw his ball as high up in the sky as possible and, as predicted, it ended up on the roof.

Bobby's father was angry that his son had done the exact opposite to his request and now Joseph would have to retrieve the ball that was stuck in the gutter.

Bobby became very quiet and withdrawn. He was a sensitive child and would often self-protect through shutting down when somebody was angry at him, especially his parents. He regretted his high-flying-ball throw, and wished he had listened to his father in the first place.

Joseph quickly calmed down and realized he had to help Bobby understand how to learn from his mistake. He let Bobby know that he understood that Bobby did not care about the ball, but he really cared about disappointing his father. Joseph just held the moment and conveyed to his sensitive son that he was understood and loved no matter what. Joseph's heart was in the right place. Eventually the moment passed and Bobby gave Joseph a big hug, and then he said something that surprised his father.

"Daddy, I love you" [no surprise], "and I never want you to die" [surprise]. Joseph wondered where that had come from. One minute they were having fun, then there was a typical parent-child moment, then it was a powerful moment of understanding between two people, and then his son feared the death of his father!

But that is the way it is with love and connection. When the ass gets out of the way and the heart feels the love, then we are free to allow both the love and the fear to exist without resistance. Essentially, when we feel truly seen and understood by somebody, and we feel their significance and value in our life, we fear losing them. It is a common reaction in children to fear the loss of a parent or loved one, especially during those moments of closeness. But it is not just children who feel this way; we all do. Children just express the fear more openly.

Inevitably, we fear losing those we love more than anything. This is why we turn things ass-backward. We try to trick ourselves with distractions. We cannot escape this vulnerability, no matter how much we try to protect and distract ourselves from inevitable loss. We cannot love without a feeling of loss being in there as well. Love and fear are always wrapped up in the same package, so we need to get the ass back in the right place and accept this so we do not run away from the moments that actually have meaning and satisfaction and can truly fill us up. It is much easier to give our attention to the moments that are not so powerful, the moments when somebody was just being human and annoyed us. We have it ass-backward when we focus more intensely on the pushy person who stole the parking spot than on loved ones where our attention actually makes a difference. It is also easier to pursue a distraction than it is for us to feel and fear the overpowering emotion that real relationships can bring.

There are so many ways to distract ourselves out there. Do you ever feel that too much of your energy is spent attending to the distractions? Although the administrative work has to get done, or that person in the lineup really was rude, there is no doubt that those moments do not hold the beauty and power of an intimate connection. In fact, as we get older, it is increasingly important to recognize that we are all mortal and the moments spent in distraction are rather costly, as they are a waste of precious time.

Humans are human and we will disappoint, hurt, and frustrate each other. There are times when we need to lighten up and let go. It is a waste to spend too much time reacting to the annoying habits of another. We need to acknowledge our frustration that the parking spot was taken by somebody else, but then we need to move on. To dwell on something is to get stuck and it quickly becomes a waste of energy. It is easy to focus our frustration on a stranger as we are not in any intimate relationship with them.

We can get it ass-backward in the significant relationships as well. If we just focus on all the annoying things that our friends, family, and partners do, we will put the ass back in charge and waste more time. If you spend enough time with any human being, you will find that there are things about that person that become annoying to you. When I say "we have it ass-backward," I mean that we not only shy away from the powerful moments of connection, but we also focus on the wrong moments.

What is the key to happiness?

I once had a client ask me what I felt was the key to happiness. Now I had a bit of a reaction to that question, as I have witnessed so many people struggle with trying to find happiness. Let's dig into the concept of happiness a bit deeper before we figure out what the key to happiness is.

I encourage you to really think about what happiness means to you, and whether happiness is something you are pursuing in your life. This word is used so freely, and happiness is so often presented as the thing you should be feeling. It might seem that if you are not happy, you must be doing something wrong.

Have you ever pretended to be happy in order to demonstrate that you have made the right decision or to justify the choice you made? But inside you were struggling with the choice and did not want to appear as if you had failed in some way? Have you ever found yourself in a situation where you should feel happy, but for some reason you just do not feel this way, and again you feel like a failure, because you did not get it right somehow? This overused and misunderstood word feeds into the ass-backward theory, as people spend a great deal of time, energy, and money trying to find happiness and satisfaction in the wrong places.

It has been my experience that people think happiness is some state they will achieve, and then all will be well in their lives when they get there. Maybe we really do have this happiness thing ass-backward as well. I ask the reader to consider that happiness might just be one emotion among many and that it can come and go like every other feeling we have. If happiness is just an emotion, it might be that we are spending our lives pursuing happiness and setting ourselves up for disappointment and frustration, as we are always in pursuit of something that is fleeting, rather than accepting and appreciating the moment we are in.

I have felt that the North American culture puts far too much emphasis on happiness, and sets an unrealistic standard in which each individual is somehow entitled to happiness, as though it were a personal right. Happiness certainly is a pleasurable emotion, so of course it makes sense that we want to feel good and, therefore, we want to feel happy. But if we approach happiness as an entitlement or the desired outcome of our life, we will become lost looking for happiness rather than experiencing the joy and intimacy of the moment in front of us. Many people are left feeling inadequate, because they have not achieved happiness or they feel dissatisfied, because they are still pursuing happiness.

When my client asked me about the key to happiness, I wanted to encourage her to rethink her perception of happiness. I replied that I was not looking for a key to happiness but rather I was encouraging people to accept the moments of joy in their lives. The actual word "enjoy" tells us what to do: we are to be "in joy" when that feeling is upon us. I told my client that I believe that satisfaction in life comes from accepting and experiencing those moments of joy. I also warned my client that we have to learn to accept and experience the other feelings that are not as enjoyable, but to let go and truly have fun in those joyful moments when they are in front of us.

The question stuck with me and I was not truly satisfied with how I had answered it. When I went home that evening, I kept thinking about the client's "key-to-happiness" question, and felt there was more to the answer.

After sleeping on it, I got up the next morning and realized what else I wanted to say. Rather than seeing it simply as happiness, I believe what we are actually looking for is a sense of satisfaction. I feel that satisfaction in life is a process and involves more than just paying attention to the moment, but rather it comes from learning what to take personally and what not to take personally. This was the crystallization of the "ass-backward theory."

We literally need to grasp those moments that are personal and allow ourselves to feel them on a deep level, because they feel so good and right when we let them in. Overall, these "real" moments might scare and overwhelm us, because there is loss and love wrapped up together, but WOW! Those moments do feel good, and by allowing them in, we are building a satisfying life! The intimate moments are not the ones to guard against, but rather we have to guard against the massive amount of energy we put into taking the wrong moments personally. To get more out of life we have to think about which emotions and situations we want to give more attention to.

Relationships ~ It's not all about you!

When we look honestly at our behaviour in relationships, and in particular our significant relationships (such as with romantic partners, parents, siblings, parents, children, dear friends), we can spend a lot of time taking the wrong things personally.

Greg and Donna

Greg and Donna are an example of how behaviour can be misinterpreted and personalized in a way that is not constructive for an exceptional life. When Greg and Donna first moved in together, they were so excited about finally having their own home and building their lives as a couple. They had dated for two years, were now in their late twenties and felt the timing was perfect. They enjoyed many of the same people and activities, and had rarely had any disagreements. During the last two years, they had both been very busy finishing their degrees, so now they would have the opportunity to really spend time in each other's company.

They had fun exploring the thrift stores for interesting and inexpensive furniture to decorate their apartment, and truly enjoyed being with each other. All their friends commented on how compatible they were and what a great home they had put together. They were both starting interesting jobs in their chosen fields, and were glad to have evenings and weekends free after years of studying and school. Both of them were serious about the relationship and felt committed to a future together.

Things began well, but neither of them knew how to communicate when something difficult would arise as they had had few disagreements and differences in their relationship. Donna found herself increasingly frustrated when Greg would go off to the spare room and play his guitar for hours. Greg was a gifted musician but had let it slip during his years of education, and now he was making up for lost time. Donna felt hurt that he could leave her for so long without explanation and that all his attention was on his guitar rather than her. She loved that he was an accomplished musician, but she did not understand how he could leave the room and not even check in with her. Every day when he picked up the guitar, she found herself resenting him and the guitar, and was soon feeling angry as soon as he approached the instrument. She interpreted Greg's focus on his music as a rejection of her.

She started dwelling on this hurt and she would then sit and stew the entire time he played and resent him for choosing his guitar over her. When Greg returned from his hours of practice, she would give him the cold shoulder, and be remote and disconnected until he pursued her to find out what was wrong.

Greg was confused by her behaviour and he would try to figure out what was wrong and why Donna was not talking to him when earlier that day they had been having such a great time. He would ask her what was wrong and she would tell him "nothing"; but he knew something was wrong and wished he could fix it. Donna was always sociable and enjoyed her time with friends, but she was increasingly booking up her time with social engagements outside the home. Greg was confused by this as she kept telling him she wanted more time with him, but then when he had time, she was not at home.

The resentment and confusion were growing and it soon hit the point where they were going to bed angry each night. They knew they loved each other but recognized they needed some assistance figuring out what was going on in their relationship.

They attended counselling and were able to quickly figure out that they were getting it ass-backward by misinterpreting each other's behaviours and taking the wrong things personally. They were also increasingly missing the moments that were meant to be personal. Donna was hurt that her vibrant personality was not enough to hold his interest. Greg was hurt that she seemed to be choosing time with her friends over him.

Greg and Donna's relationship is an example of the time, energy, and disconnect that can occur when one approaches things ass-backward and the focus is on the wrong things.

She was taking his need for his own space and creative time as a statement on her value. It actually had nothing to do with her value and was not personal at all! There are a whole lot of moments in this life where it is not all about us!

He was taking her need to connect with other people as a rejection of him, when in fact Donna was an extroverted person and she just enjoyed spending time with people. We all need to remind ourselves of this. Greg and Donna learned to let each other know when they wanted each other's attention and stopped punishing each other for not being able to read each other's minds. As they came to understand what not to take personally, they were no longer threatened by the times they each needed time and space to do other things and connect with other people. Once they understood this, they were able to communicate very effectively and build a satisfying and joyful life together. Greg and Donna are still going strong and by learning how to embrace the truly personal moments, they have taken a huge step toward exceptional living.

Step #4 ~ Accept the Human Moments

Humans seem to struggle with just allowing each other our humanity. Part of this may be our desire for perfection, or the unrealistic expectations we build, or just because we want to have something to dwell upon. We will all trigger somebody, or be triggered by somebody. We are often not even aware that our action has triggered a reaction. There are also times when we are aware of this and we are looking for a reaction. Then there are times when we just want an excuse to behave poorly. The thing to understand is that when we do behave poorly, it is usually not personal. These are just our "human moments" when we make mistakes and we are not at our best. We all have these moments.

In my home, we try to admit that we all have "human moments" and that we will all make mistakes with each other. I know that after a long day at the office where I have had to deal with some challenging situations; I might be grumpy and short-tempered with my family. This is not a good excuse for bad behaviour, and in the end, it is best to take responsibility for my actions, but all of us at some point have dumped our bad moods on others.

If we can recognize that the other person is in a grumpy mood, is having a bad day, or is distracted or discouraged, and not take it personally, we can then respond in a way that is non-defensive and can actually shift the energy of the situation. If we take somebody else's bad mood personally and get agitated or defensive ourselves we are making things ass-backward again, and putting a lot of time and energy into something that takes us farther and farther away from true connection with another person.

All in all, as humans, we tend to spend a lot of time dwelling on the moments that were not meant to be personal, and if we are being honest with ourselves, it is a waste of energy.

When taking the steps to exceptional living we need to recognize, as often as possible, that others will dump their moods and bad days on us at times and we will dump on others as well. It will just happen with anybody you are close to. Avoid getting it ass-backward and getting caught up in reacting to somebody else's reactivity. This does not mean that we should not stand up for ourselves; it means that our responses are usually much more powerful when they are non-defensive. Conflict can be resolved much more quickly when one speaks one's own truth without attacking or defending.

Emotional Pain

As this chapter explains, the ass-backward theory is an illustration of how our modern emotional distress comes from trying to protect against pain rather than just feeling it. Sometimes we act as if emotional pain is going to kill us. We often approach emotional pain with the same sort of "alarm" as physical pain. As a species, humans appear to be acting as if we cannot turn off our alarm buttons. We construct all sorts of defences so that we will not feel the deep pain and fear, but in fact we are creating a multitude of emotional problems and pain because of the mechanisms we build to avoid the pain. Again, we have this all a bit ass-backward.

I often find myself reminding people that emotional pain will not kill them and that the real danger lies in avoiding the pain. I am not saying that emotional pain and depression have not contributed to deaths and suicides; I am saying that life ends due to a physical cause and not simply from emotional pain. I am not minimizing how devastating it can feel to have a broken heart, or to experience loss and betrayal, but our fighting against these does not help us in the end. We still feel pain and frustration; we just have to be careful that we do not distract ourselves with drama and turmoil about things that are not so important and that we have no control over anyway, and accept that the things that are important will make us vulnerable to emotional pain.

Anxiety

Anxiety is also part of the ass-backward theory, as it is our alarm system. Since we are programmed for fight or flight and our alarm gets triggered if we feel an emotional or physical vulnerability, we are experiencing this alarm as anxiety and stress.

There is no doubt that anxiety can cause things to go "ass-backward" and it takes a bit of work to get things back in alignment. Nevertheless, getting your life back in order is highly achievable, as long as we remember to watch for the pointers along the path and recognize those moments when we are concentrating on the wrong things. If we can allow ourselves to be human, aim to treat ourselves and others with respect, but also forgive each other when we inevitably mess up, then we can focus our energy back on what is truly substantial and important in our lives.

Questions for Contemplation

What techniques do you use to protect yourself from emotional pain?

Who do you most fear being emotionally hurt by?

Have you ever found yourself overreacting to a situation or person who was not that important to you? Did you understand why you reacted this way?

Have you ever found yourself feeling overwhelmed by how much you love somebody?

Do you feel that love and loss are connected?

What relationships do you value the most?

Do you think you spend too much time with distractions?

What are your distractions?

What brings you joy?

Do you feel that moments of joy and happiness are the same thing or different?

Do you forgive yourself your human moments?

Do you forgive others quickly, or do you hold onto the hurt?

Do you agree that it is human to disappoint each other?

When called out on a behaviour do you try to listen to the other person, or do you focus on how to respond and defend yourself?

What are your top three priorities in your life?

CHAPTER FIVE

Engage with Your Life; Be Present for Yourself in Your Life; Get in Your Life; It is the Only Life You Have.

"Even in Kyoto Hearing the cuckoo's cry I long for Kyoto"
Matuao Bosho (1644-1694)

It is a common struggle to learn how to be present and pay attention to the moment we are in. To illustrate this, I will share a little of my own journey of awareness. A light bulb moment came when I was invited to a friend's home for a social evening and caught sight of a black and white photo of a Japanese city that was strikingly simple and elegant. As I removed my shoes and made to join the gathering, I was immediately drawn to the picture. I moved in closer so that I could take a better look at it and read the words that were at the bottom. They read, "Here I Am in Kyoto Wishing I Was in Kyoto," a simplification of the Haiku above. To me, both the quote and the Haiku mean, "Here I am in my exceptional life wishing I were in my exceptional life."

A Haiku is a form of Japanese poetry in which the writer is limited to seventeen syllables and needs to structure the syllables in three lines of five, seven, and then five. The impact of that simple structure and sparse words was astounding for me that night. The rest of that evening's socializing is a vague and pleasant memory, but the feeling that I had when I read those words is as clear now as the moment I read them.

Why was this so powerful and profound to me? It was as if I recognized a tendency to disconnect from the moment within myself and I felt these simple words applied to a greater human truth, not just to me. We could be right where we wish to be, and still disconnect from the moment and the place. Those words immediately became a part of my philosophy of life, but they also dipped into a deeper yearning to learn how to truly appreciate and enjoy this amazing gift of life. From that moment on, I began a conscious personal quest. I also wanted to understand how we as humans could overcome this predisposition to check out and miss the beauty and joy that is right in front of us.

Step #5 ~ Quiet the Chatter

In general, we strive to better ourselves. Many people are looking to enhance and make the most of their lives. The human brain has a highly developed prefrontal cortex and this allows us to engage in complex thinking. This ability for creative thought is at the root of much of human ingenuity, but this area of the brain also leads us to indulge in a great deal of chatter and distraction and forget to actually pay attention to the moment.

Sarah

When I first met Sarah, she was somebody who often got distracted by all the chatter around her. She is a twenty-nine-year-old woman who sought counselling shortly after she got married. Sarah had always wanted to get married. She had been dreaming about her wedding day ever since she started school. She wanted it to be the best of all days. When she met Matthew in university and fell in love, she knew she was going to marry him. Matthew truly was a great match for Sarah and the wedding date was set. Sarah had everything planned, right down to the tiniest detail. She was very successful and high functioning and had an active and creative mind, so she enjoyed coordinating all the preparations.

The big day finally arrived and everything was just as she had planned. The venue was perfect, the guests had arrived, she looked fabulous, Matthew was handsome, and best of all he was in love with her. All went well and the wedding was beautiful, but there was one significant problem for Sarah. As the day progressed, she felt more and more disconnected. She was struggling to stay present in this very important day.

There were many things that contributed to this. She was exhausted, overwhelmed by the actual day and had spent so much time in her head before the big event, that she was not sure how to spend the day in her body. She loved Matthew very much and did not regret anything about marrying him; she was just disappointed that she "checked out" on her big day.

Sarah reported that she was grateful for her good life and did not classify herself as unhappy, but she had always struggled with some anxiety and her ability to feel engaged in the moment. She often found that she could not stop her mind from whirling in all sorts of directions. Sarah had trouble sleeping and letting go of things and just did not know how to quiet the chatter. The work Sarah did in her counselling sessions was not problem-based work, but rather resource-building work, so that Sarah could "get out of her head" sometimes and just experience the joy in her life. She understood that counselling was about building skills and she was open to learning new techniques that would assist her in living an exceptional life.

So the struggle for Sarah and many others is, "Here I am, in my life, not quite able to be in my life." The challenge is learning to be more mindful of the moment in front of us. There are many times when we should be appreciating and enjoying the life we are in, but we get distracted by the chatter and we just autopilot through the experience. We all recognize the moment when we can be so deeply in thought that we autopilot our vehicle right past our exit, and realize too late that we missed our opportunity to turn. Sometimes we do that same thing in other parts of our lives as well.

When Sarah told me her story about her wedding, I reassured her that everyone finds themselves operating on autopilot at times. I used the MORE philosophy to help her understand herself better and to transform a disappointment into growth. She came to understand that there are benefits in having an effective autopilot as it could assist her with relaxation and creative thoughts. She just needed skills to turn off the autopilot and pay attention to the road she was on. She also saw how her "checking out" on an important day was actually an opportunity and reminder to build this awareness in her life. She needed to be realistic with herself; there were times she was filling her life so full that she was not leaving much space or time for awareness.

Opportunities are a cornerstone of the MORE philosophy and although we cannot embrace every opportunity we encounter, it helps to recognize them as they arise. Some opportunities might not cross our paths again, and if we do not pay attention, we lose that choice. To get things done, we do need to focus on the job at hand, but we also need to refresh our minds and connections, and allow ourselves to just enjoy the moment. Even on the best of days in an exceptional life, it is likely that you will still struggle with this dilemma! To just sit and absorb and accept the moment is a challenge. Your mind might race to a work issue, your financial responsibilities, and your relationship with a friend, to just about everywhere except where you are!

Ohmmmm!

On my quest to stay in the moment and assist myself and others in appreciating the beautiful surroundings of life, I enthusiastically took every professional training I could in order to build an effective tool box. I pursued training in meditation and hypnosis as I felt these skills would be great tools. I soon found for me that meditation was not as easy as it looked.

While doing the practice portions of the meditation training in which we were guided to free our minds of worry and follow

the breathing exercises, I began to feel as if I were missing something that everyone else seemed to be getting. I would look out
the corner of my eye at all the other counsellors who appeared
so relaxed and I envied them their meditative state, and started to
think that there must be something wrong with my approach as
I sure did not feel relaxed.

My mind became hyper-alert and frustrated because I could not
free and clear it. The more the instructor practised meditation
with us, the more I felt like a fake. I was practically praying for
the meditation exercises to be over, as I felt I was just moments
away from losing it altogether. I pretended to reach my happy
place and endured the meditation.

How could I assist others if I could not even do these simple
exercises that seemed to come so naturally to others?

In fact, the attempts to meditate appeared to increase my
anxiety rather than decrease it. For example, I would go into
the meditation classes somewhat at ease, and I would come out
feeling inadequate and a little neurotic because I could not do it
correctly. It got to the point where I just felt anxious thinking
about the classes; so I thought for the time being that I had better give up the pursuit of a "Zen-like state" and look for some
other tools. As it was I knew that I could not handle the anxiety
of meditating daily; if I wanted a successful practice and good
mental health I was going to have to give up this pursuit of a free
and clear mind.

I found other ways of dealing with stress and eventually found
some relaxation techniques that were helpful to me. Now this
little diatribe is not a stance against meditation, as I believe it is a
powerful tool for some and a truly healthy way of life for others.
It is just that my initial struggle with meditation illustrates that
things need to be authentic for each person and there is no guar-
antee that what works for one will work for another. I was just
not able to quiet the mental chatter with meditation at that time
in my life. The problem was that I was approaching meditation
as a perfectionist and trying to follow a technique rather than

finding a way to integrate the experience in order to make it real for me. But my relationship with meditation was not over yet.

This brings me back to the moment of reading the Haiku on the wall at the party. I knew I had a "busy" mind that was both a gift and a curse, as it could easily distract me from truly being where I was at any particular time. I also knew that life was an incredible gift and I quite enjoyed my active mind, but I wanted to learn to quiet it at times and be present mentally and physically in my exceptional life.

The Mindfulness Movement eventually emerged in the therapy world. This is a school of thought that explores how to be present through meditation, relaxation, breathing, and an understanding of the neuropsychology of the brain. There is new fascinating brain science out there that helps us understand the workings of the brain, how we can optimize our brain potential, and how we can enhance our well-being through an understanding of our mind. Mindfulness also provides techniques to help one focus on being present and gaining a sense of self. Through Mindfulness training, I discovered that I actually can meditate, but I need to do it in a way that fits my approach. One of my realizations was that I was going about the whole meditation thing ass-backward by approaching it simply as a technique for the tool box that needed to be mastered. By trying to clear my mind as if it were a task, I was setting myself up for failure. I was focusing my energy on trying to do it right, as opposed to just allowing the moment.

My mind is a busy place, and rather than fight it I needed to accept the thoughts as they arose. If I recognize these thoughts, honor my active mind, and then just move back to my centre, I find that this works for me. I did not need to lie on the floor or sit cross-legged at an ashram, but rather I needed to take a few minutes and just focus on my centre.

For me, the place of focus is my chest, as this feels like my centre. Maybe this is where my mind, my spirit, my heart, and my inner self sit in my body. I no longer try to fight the thoughts, and this is such a relief. I can enjoy my mind, and even be amused by some of my thoughts, and then move gently back to my centre.

This helps me to be present and I can do it in a couple of minutes, which I must admit works for me in my busy life. I cannot always find a quiet place to collect myself, but I have been able to develop an ever-increasing ability to take a couple of moments anywhere and collect myself by concentrating on my centre, without battling my thoughts.

I have also come to enjoy these moments of quiet when I have them and extend my meditation practice as it feels true to me. This simple technique has assisted me in not just wishing I were here, but in actually realizing that I am here right now. My ability to be in the moment is readily available to me, and all I have to do is be aware. There are times though that I just need to recognize that I have wandered off, and look for the pointers that will then bring me back to the path.

If you have ever drifted off and missed out on a conversation then you may understand this struggle. Have you ever had trouble focusing on a beautiful moment because you were thinking of something else? Have you ever driven right past the turn to your house? Have you ever felt that you somehow missed out on an important event in your life because you checked out? If you answered yes to any of these questions, you may find the following exercises helpful.

The MORE Philosophy Meditation

Take a minute to become aware of your body and your surroundings.

Do not feel obliged to sit on the floor or lie down, but if you have the time and inclination you can do so. Just get comfortable wherever you are.

Close your eyes if you would like.

Take a deep breath in, hold it for four seconds and then let it out slowly. Breathe in, hold, breathe out, breathe in, hold, and breathe out. Continue this rhythm of breathing, but allow yourself to feel natural.

Become aware of your thoughts. Allow them to emerge.

Welcome your thoughts and any feelings that accompany them. Acknowledge them and honour them.

Let your thoughts go and return to the place in your body that feels like your centre.

Imagine yourself in a safe or special place in which you feel relaxed and healthy.

Allow your thoughts to come again, and return to your centre and the image of yourself feeling relaxed and healthy.

Allow yourself to be aware of the movement around you.

Allow yourself to be aware of the movement within your body.

Follow the movement of your breath through your body.

This moment is the opportunity to just be you, nothing else, just you.

This moment is real, and it is exceptional just like you.

Do this for as long or as short a time as you want.

The MORE Philosophy Five-Senses Check-In

The MORE Philosophy Five-Senses Check-In is another simple way to get back in the moment and experience your exceptional life when you find your mind wandering. This involves a quick check in with each one of your five physical senses. You can do this anytime and anywhere you want. It is helpful for all of us to take a moment now and again to collect ourselves. A natural and easy way of doing this is the following:

What do I smell right now?

(Example answer: I smell the fresh air and some flowers.)

What do I see right now?

(Example answer: I see the trees outside my window and the sun shining on my desk.)

What do I hear right now?

(Example answer: I hear the sound of people talking, some music in the background, my children laughing.)

What do I taste right now?

(Example answer: I taste the coffee still lingering in my mouth.)

What do I feel physically right now?

(Example answer: I feel the warmth of the day, the chair pressing into my back, and my feet on the ground. I feel like I may need to stretch soon and walk around to enjoy this beautiful moment in this beautiful life.)

MORE Philosophy Breaks

Get up and stretch, even if you only have a second.
Go for a walk and check out your surroundings.
Change activities once in a while to keep yourself alert.
If something is bothering you and you cannot get it off your mind, write it down and then put it away.
Do something that is creative, listen to music, write, draw, or do any other activity that will assist you in changing your pace once in a while.

Step #6 ~ Accept the Good with the Bad

So now that we have recognized that it may help to have some techniques to train ourselves to be in the moment and appreciate and enjoy this life, there is an additional complication.

Sometimes being in the moment is not where we want to be. I guess this step could be called, "Here I am in Kyoto wishing I were somewhere else!" The story of Brenda and her much-anticipated vacation may help illustrate that we have to accept the good with the bad in order to live an exceptional life.

Brenda

Brenda had booked a week at a nice resort in a tropical location for herself and her family and she could hardly wait. It was November in Vancouver, a great time to get away from the wet and the rain. Prior to going on the holiday, she had worked exceptionally long hours to allow herself freedom from her responsibilities while she was away. She had been practising the

MORE Philosophy Meditation and the Five-Sense Check-in, and she was ready to make every moment count.

When she first arrived, she was almost overwhelmed by the experience. It was such a beautiful place and she could hardly believe she was there. It seemed so strange to have woken up early that morning in rainy Vancouver and to be on a beach on the other side of the continent in a different country only hours later. She did her meditation and kept checking in with her five senses and soon she was able to settle into the space and time she was in.

Brenda felt she had truly arrived! But now that she had arrived, life was about to teach her another lesson.

As she settled in and became connected with all her surroundings and senses, she realized she was not feeling well. As each day passed, she felt worse and worse. Her symptoms did not make sense to her. She was experiencing severe pain in her ear; she had a huge headache; and the rest of her body was filled with aching.

She kept on going as she was a determined person and she wanted to be present with her family during this once-in-a-lifetime experience. She participated in all the excursions she had planned, but as each day passed, her energy decreased. She tried to ignore the pain and discomfort but she could not.

On their last night at the resort, the family went for a dinner on the beach, and she finally admitted to herself how much pain she was in. She knew this was her last evening in the tropical paradise, so she forced herself to be present and watch the beautiful scene as the sun set into the ocean.

The sunset and the physical surroundings were truly magnificent! Picture perfect! She felt like laughing and crying at the same time as she was certainly feeling present in her life and aware of the beauty around her, but she would rather be home and in bed and not having to deal with all this beauty.

Once she returned home, she saw her doctor and was diagnosed with shingles. She now had to deal with recovering from shingles and her disappointment of feeling so sick on her holiday.

I assisted Brenda in understanding that being present means more than just appreciating the moment one is in. The hard truth is that to be present in life means you will also experience both pain and challenges. The pain and beauty in life can be all mixed up together, just like the moment Brenda watched the sunset and felt those conflicting emotions.

When we are present in the moment, the joy and the pain in our lives might be heightened. When we are honest with what we are feeling, the sensations might run deeper. We do not achieve the perfect moment, but rather we accept all that the moment offers. If we can accept this, we will not run away from pain so quickly; we will understand that we can endure the pain and that it will pass.

In order to get through some of the tough moments, we have to forge through the pain. I am not encouraging that we dwell on the pain, or that we need to fully experience every sensation of pain. What I am encouraging is that we are honest with ourselves about the pain, rather than trying to deny its existence. Not every moment is meant to be an eleven and there will be some that require you to go off to bed and rest to heal; others might require that you dig deep and pull on all of your strength and endurance to get to the next step.

An exceptional life will have many painful experiences that you will need to push yourself through in order to meet your obligations or the goals you have set. Recognizing pain does not mean we give into pain and give up, but it is the moments that we are honest with ourselves that are the most vivid, meaningful, and informative. Those moments of honesty can point us along the path that directs our next steps.

An exceptional life will be filled with rich moments, and if we want the "full-meal deal," there will be times we will get more than we bargained for and times when we get less than we counted on. Life just works this way. To only accept the beautiful and joyful moments means you will limit your experience. To accept the moments with all their beauty and challenges means you will get all the information you need and you will actually feel yourself living an exceptional life filled with exceptional moments. Sometimes we will have to accept the day as it comes and savour the moments that we can. If we have more moments of being in Kyoto than not, let's call that progress.

Questions for Contemplation

Where do you feel most relaxed in your life?

Do you find yourself operating on autopilot often?

What is the image in your mind when you think of a safe and relaxed place?

What does relaxation feel like in your body?

How do you nurture and take care of yourself?

Do you take time to check in with yourself on a daily basis?

Which of your senses is your most dominant?

How do you deal with physical pain?

How do you express joy in your life?

CHAPTER SIX

Be Authentic and Truthful with Yourself; Facilitate Honest Conversations.

"Time To Be Honest With Yourself and Cut through the Bullshit!"

It is my experience that one of the great challenges in life is being honest. Although honesty with others is at times a tricky business, it seems to me that honesty with oneself is an even greater challenge. If we really want an exceptional life, we are going to need to cut through the bullshit we tell ourselves.

The reason we avoid the truth in this manner is to protect our vulnerabilities and sensitivities. None of us want to feel pain and discomfort, but if we can accept that this is part of the deal, then we can begin to be honest with ourselves.

There really is no easy way to put this. I struggled with whether I should use the word "bullshit" as I wrote about this essential step. In the end, I felt the need to call it what it is. We have built too much of our lives on misperceptions and the bullshit that we tell ourselves. If we are using justifications and excuses as a foundation for our lives there is no doubt we will struggle with some "shit" along the way. Again, I am not pushing for purity and perfection here. I am pushing for honesty, authenticity, and straight talk. If we want to have authentic relationships with those around us, we must first have an authentic relationship with ourselves.

One of the pillars of health in any relationship is trust and honesty. I believe that the best connections are those that feel authentic and real. The more real you are in a relationship, the more true the connection. I encourage people to hold onto who they are and speak their truths in relationships, but this type of honesty should not be an excuse for brutal criticism of another, nor is it meant to be an excuse to behave poorly.

We are much better at pointing out the flaws and failings of others, and in our self-protection we quickly point the finger the other way rather than at ourselves. There is not a lot of growth in this type of approach to life, communication, and relationships.

We can move toward an exceptional life if we can take an approach that requires us to look at our own conduct and then learn from our own mistakes and missteps. It is also beneficial to learn from the mistakes of others, and some of us are able to learn by observation, but there is no doubt that the most powerful learning of all is from our own experience. It is also the most powerful challenge.

How do we preserve our sense of worth and dignity, and still learn from our mistakes? How do we preserve another's dignity in the face of their mistakes, and how can we all learn from each other?

Step #7 ~ Learn from your Mistakes

Mistakes

If you are human you will make mistakes and mess up. In fact, it is my belief that these mistakes are interwoven with our purpose in life. One of the main principles of the MORE Philosophy is recognizing that mistakes are some of the most fruitful opportunities of all. It is through these opportunities that we grow and learn what we are made of and what we have to contribute. If someone fears their mistakes they will put their energy into covering up, or distracting people from the mistakes. Through the years, and through some truly humbling experiences, I have come to believe that mistakes are essential to an exceptional life.

These flaws and fumbles add character, and the imperfections bond us together as a human race. When I know that you too have been humbled and are imperfect, I can relax my guard and expose my true self and my imperfections as well.

Lessons

Without mistakes and missteps, there are no interesting stories, and no place for our lives to intersect and truly connect with others. My son once said to me when he was he was around nine years old, "Mom, there are no good stories without a problem."

Not only was I impressed by his intuitive understanding of storytelling, but I also thought that he was correct. All the most interesting stories I am aware of are based on problems of some sort. I believe part of the human experience is that each and every one of us is presented with a series of problems that we are given opportunities to overcome. In our own unique story there appear significant challenges that can highly elevate us if overcome, or destroy us if ignored. If we ignore or defend our mistakes, we miss the opportunity to transform this challenge into a great triumph.

It is in our best interest to recognize the mistake as quickly as possible. If we keep repeating the mistakes, they become bigger and costlier in order to get our attention. Life is generous and will always send another opportunity for us to transform this challenge, but each lesson will be bigger and more dramatic and require more humbling. If we never take these opportunities, the challenge might even destroy us in the end. At the base of this challenge is a fear; if we let our fear win, we will not learn from our mistakes, nor will we achieve the exceptional life we could be living. So we need to accept the humanness within ourselves and others. We will fail, we will make mistakes, and we will mess things up. We are not perfect, and we are not expected to be perfect. Perfection is stagnant and boring anyway! There is no movement in perfection. There will always be some parts of ourselves that remain flawed, and some parts that will grow.

For instance, I will never be a mathematician. I have accepted my math dyslexia as a rather interesting part of myself. It pushed me to find creative solutions to the math problems I struggled with in high school and even in university. It helped me build resiliency and adaptability that I have been able to apply to many areas of my life. My flaw prompted me to grow. Now that I have done my time with math class and developed creative ways to compensate, I no longer need to struggle with this particular issue. The reality of the MORE philosophy is I will not be studying trigonometry on the side for fun, although I might enjoy a book about Greek civilization and the great minds that developed math and astronomy equations.

The Blueprint

Each of us has a list of our challenges and blocks, as well as a list of our strengths and gifts. If we can accept this information, we can start to see the reality of the blueprint that is there. Take an inventory and have an honest conversation by asking yourself the following questions.

- What are my strengths?
- What are my challenges?
- What are my gifts?
- What are my blocks?
- What do I need to learn from my challenges?
- When do I most need my strengths?
- What makes me interesting?
- Where do I want to spend my time and energy?

The Promise

I remember a moment in time when I had an honest conversation that changed a perception I had held for a long time. Because of this conversation, I moved from something that did not feel quite real to something that felt very real–from the romanticist to the realist.

Let me set the stage. It was a truly romantic evening right down to the subdued lighting in the room. My boyfriend and I had recently got engaged and we were sitting in front of the fireplace discussing the plans for our wedding. The music was playing in the background and the moment was almost perfect. We might have even had candles and incense.

Although I was always a very practical and pragmatic person, there was the young romantic in me who wanted a great love story (remember the ones filled with drama and problems?). My fiancé Bruce told me that he was going to make me a promise. The promise he made me that night has always stayed close to my heart and my mind. It truly became a part of the fabric of our relationship.

We were sitting and talking and sharing that romantic moment planning our future together and he said to me, "I will make you a promise going into this marriage."

I was excited. What was he going to promise me? His never-ending love? His undying commitment to our marriage? To be my knight in shining armour forever? Well that is not what he promised me.

Instead, he said to me, "I promise you that I will make mistakes. I promise you that I will disappoint you. I promise you that I will bring myself to this marriage, and I will let you do the same."

Now, this was not what I expected. In that first romantic swell I was disappointed in his promise: (as he had predicted, I would be disappointed in him), but within a couple of minutes, I understood the depth of the commitment he was making. I also understood the beauty and authenticity of what he was telling me. We could be human together, we were bound to make mistakes, and hopefully we would be able to accept and forgive each other our disappointments.

He was offering me a real love, not a romantic built up love filled with roses and empty promises. He courageously identified himself as a real person who understood he was not perfect, was rather scared to expose his imperfections, but was ready to take the next step. He was offering me the opportunity to be real and flawed as well. It made me realize I was bound to disappoint him as well, and I was going to have to deal with my own discomfort with mistakes and imperfections.

As I look back, I realize he was giving me the opportunity to live an exceptional life – the MORE philosophy was already becoming part of my marriage.

I still count that moment as one of my favourite memories. I feel that by accepting his promise I was also ready for the next step, which was a move toward a grown-up relationship, built on reality with two very imperfect humans who were ready to take a chance on each other. In the end, this is probably the most romantic thing we can do for each other. Although I wished for romantic love, an undying love, and a hero, I was offered a real man with real fears. The interesting thing is he has given me all the things I wished for and there is no doubt he is my hero and loves me in the way I wanted and needed to be loved, but all this came in a very real human package.

I would never go back and change that moment. Although it was not what I wanted to hear in that instant, it was exactly what I needed to hear and I will always cherish his honesty and courage in that moment. There was no "bullshit" in that moment. It was an honest conversation between two very human people. It truly warms my imperfect heart every time I think of it. It also inspired me to be honest. All in all, it was an important reality check about an important decision and event in my life, and it illustrates the power of authentic imperfection.

In my work as a counsellor with couples and families I encourage people who are in love and committing themselves to each other to also consider their reality checks. Be careful if you base your relationship on romantic ideals and promises of what you wish and who you wish you were. Don't buy a load of bullshit just because it is covered in roses! In the end the roses will wash away and it is still just bullshit. Rather, look to the real promise that allows you to grow and thrive and develop an exceptional relationship.

A wedding can be a great celebration filled with love, beauty, and romance, but the foundation of a relationship such as a marriage needs to be built on reality, as well as honesty with oneself and others. Again, I encourage couples to build a practical and purposeful structure, but with lots of room inside for creativity, vision, passion and love.

Step #8 ~ Stop Making Excuses

People need to build a solid structure in their lives, but many people are behaving as if they are much too fragile these days. All the psychobabble out there has not made us stronger. I am afraid that many have used the language of self-help and psychology as an excuse for poor behaviour and the reason that they are not able to make their dreams come true. Some of the common excuses which have moved their way into our culture through the language of victimhood are, "It was my parents' fault," and "I came from a dysfunctional family," and "I was not getting my needs met," and "Somebody hurt my feelings."

I am not arguing the legitimacy of these issues or minimizing anybody's pain and struggle, but I do not think using this pain as an excuse will lead toward anything exceptional. We have all experienced pain and disappointment in our lives. When these explanations are used as excuses, then the motivation is to protect the fragile ego rather than to grow through adversity.

Making excuses is very different from telling your story. Excuses are when we do not take responsibility for ourselves. Some people become very good at using a certain level of psychological awareness to talk their way out of being responsible for their own lives. Thus, they avoid the reality checks and the resiliency required to build opportunities that lie within the difficult situations they face. Making excuses does not align with the MORE philosophy.

In the psychological field, we need to be careful that we do not embed people deeper into their excuses and feed a culture of victimization. Although most of us have been victims of something at some time, we need to feel the feelings, move through ones that are associated with this event, and then focus on the growth opportunity rather than getting stuck in victimhood. There is nothing exceptional in being a victim of your own life! This is not always the politically correct way of looking at things but if we stick to political correctness we will only speak to others in a bland and "correct" manner, thus avoiding telling ourselves and others the truths we need to hear.

Time for a Reality Check

Let's do a reality check and use our insight to be honest. Let's avoid excuses and getting lost in feeling victimized. Let's take a real look at ourselves and start the honest conversation within first. We need to apply insight to evaluate and understand our strengths and assets. We can apply this reality check to our talents to better understand where to put our energy and which goals to pursue. Sometimes, we desire to be very accomplished at something, when in fact we may only be moderately talented in this area. We get our desire mixed up with reality and start to convince ourselves about what we want rather than who we are. We need to believe that who we are is enough. Who we are, with our imperfections, is actually who we are meant to be. We can strive to be our best self, but it is a waste of time to try to be somebody we are not in order to pursue a dream that does not suit us.

If I had built my marriage on a romantic ideal rather than on reality, I am not sure if it would have weathered the storms. This is true for any romantic dream we have. Our visions need to be able to weather the storms of reality. This also applies to when we pursue an interest, talent or a career. If it is not based on a solid structure, a romantic or idealistic dream can become a problem by keeping you away from your exceptional life.

Let's take the situation of a piano player who is of moderate talent. If this pianist wants to be a professional musician, she will need to have a real sense of how talented she is. This does not mean that she cannot be a professional musician if she has only moderate talent; what it means is if she wants to become an accomplished musician and actually make a career as a pianist, she had better get ready for some hard work. That is the reality check. The pianist can still accomplish this, as long as she is honest with herself and prepared to do the work. She cannot accomplish the goal of being a professional musician if she keeps telling herself that she is incredibly talented and that her lack of success is because nobody understands her and how talented she is.

The next reality check is that nobody wants to pay money to listen to any musician who is not proficient at their instrument, who never really practises, and who mopes around feeling sorry for herself. That is somebody headed for a pretty unexceptional life, and she certainly will not become an exceptional piano player. It's also the bullshit referred to in the title of this chapter! We are, however, willing to pay our money to see a musician who has put in the hours and really knows how to play their instrument.

The North American Lie

There is a great big lie out there, and nobody really wants to admit it or talk about it. Our North American society in particular has groomed a whole generation of people on this lie. We look at "the American dream" of how anybody can accomplish their dreams in the land of opportunity if they work hard enough. There is some truth in the power of hard work, but there is also a big lie and a missing piece of information in "the American dream" of success. We need to bring the reality check back to this dream. This is perfectionism at work, rather than the realism of MORE.

Hard work does pay off, but not everybody can be anything they want to be, nor should they be. We are not entitled to live out our dreams and fantasies. We need to understand our strengths and assets, and see what we can contribute in this world. The modern lie of "you can be anything you want to be" is just that: a false fable that can take you right to disappointment and disillusionment. It is a nice fable as it appeals to all of us. In this fable, anybody that works hard enough gets the prize, but that is not how reality works.

Although it is not politically correct, we need to stop telling our young people that they can do anything they want in this world; because not everybody can be anything they want to be! There are many factors that influence and direct success, and you are not in control of all those factors. Not everybody is meant to be a rock star, nor is everybody able to be a successful CEO of a large company. Not every little girl grows up to be a doctor, and not every little boy grows up to play professional sports.

We do not need an entire society of the same dreams and hopes, but rather a land of opportunity in which each unique individual has the potential for fulfillment through personal expression and service to something bigger than just their own dream. We cannot be anything we want to be, but rather we can discover our passion and find out what we can truly contribute to this world. With hard work and realistic expectations, we can achieve great things. These things are realties, not the fantasies of a young, romantic mind.

Satisfaction and success do not necessarily come from being what you "want" to be, as this is a very childlike way of looking at things, but rather from allowing yourself to develop through honesty and awareness, and then contributing that which is within you. The good news in all this is that you are enough. Essentially, you have it in you to contribute your special spark to the world and live an exceptional life, but you have to be prepared to work hard at bringing the best you have to the table.

Unfortunately, reality is not fair, nor is it politically correct; if it were, most of us would be living our glamorous lives surrounded by the rewards of our dazzling successes. If we got everything we wanted we would remain immature and underdeveloped, and we would not have much to contribute to those around us. I believe we are meant to live our own lives, but in order to do so in an exceptional manner through using the MORE philosophy, we are going to have to be honest about ourselves. This honesty starts with a reality check around the assets we possess, as well as the challenges that each of us may need to strive to overcome.

Let's revisit music as a talent. Yes, there is the possibility of success if you work hard enough, but you also have to have an honest sense of your true talent and the drive required to pursue this goal. A musician needs to ask himself, "Is this something that evokes a passion in me and do I want to commit thousands of hours to it, or do I just like the idea of being a rock star who lives in a palatial home with all the girls who want to date me?"

It is natural to have the superstar fantasy, but we need to understand that it is a fantasy. If you have a true passion for the guitar and you are prepared to do the hard work, the fantasy of the palatial home and rock star lifestyle is not that important. What is really important is the passion and excitement you feel when you play guitar, write a song, or form a band. If you do not have a true passion for the guitar, you are more likely to get your palatial home by finding the thing inside that really ignites your passion, rather than just pursuing the external rewards of success and glamour.

In keeping with the musical theme of talent, this reality-check concept can be further understood by examining three different types of guitar players. The first musician is the one who has committed his life to the pursuit of this art form. He may be a very successful rock star or he may be a session musician who plays professionally and teaches guitar on the side. The commonality is the love and commitment to the music and the craft. We are impressed with the musician who has pushed himself and creates great music through a blend of talent, practice, and musical understanding. By and large, the general public is not even aware of how much is natural talent; we are just interested in the end result and how the music makes us feel.

Now we come to the second type of guitar player. He is curious and has some interest in guitar, and he finds that he may not be as driven or talented at it as he had hoped. He just may want to learn to play guitar, as it is an enjoyable thing to do, but has no aspirations of making a career of it or spending too much time on it. If the passion is not there, his guitar-playing may fall to the side and his energy may become focused on something else that truly excites him. This is okay. It is good to try different things.

It is good to stay curious, but the reality is that you are not going to become a master at everything you try. Take chances in life and try different things, but avoid drifting without discipline. Drifting without direction and commitment leads to nowhere. We need to keep building our strengths through experiences that will require some risk to our egos. It is important to try a variety of things but it is also important to become good at something in this world. At some point, you need to push yourself, to master something to the best of your ability, as that experience will build strength, character, and discipline.

But to the guitar player who only has a moderate interest, it is unlikely that the guitar will be the thing he masters. It is likely that he may pick up a guitar once in a while and try to pluck out a tune; the guitar will not be central to his life.

The third guitarist may find she plays guitar as a creative outlet, approaching it with passion and being willing to commit some substantial time to it, yet has no desire to make it a career. She may pursue it because it excites and enhances her life, but she may not be willing to put in the thousands of hours that it takes to become a professional musician. This does not mean that music will not be at her core, but the pursuit of music as her prime income will not necessarily drive her life.

Bruce

Bruce always had musical talent. As a child he took classical training on the clarinet, but then gave that up in high school to become a "rock god." He always had a natural understanding and talent with music. He formed a band in high school and they managed to get a couple of gigs, but although each member of the band had talent, things did not take off. Their band was not highly organized and they lacked the discipline to turn it into a professional path. At one point, Bruce even gave up guitar completely, abandoning his dream of being a "rock god" and using the excuse that he could never live up to the truly brilliant jazz musicians that he listened to.

But his story with music was not over. He surrounded himself with a large music library and listened to live music whenever he got the chance. Music remained at his core and was always a passion for him. Eventually he received a second-hand guitar as a gift for Christmas. Gone were the fantasies of becoming a rock star, but the reality of a musician was there. He always had the talent, now he was ready to start working at it. He put in the hours and improved on his talent through hard work and commitment, and he has long since moved up from that humble second hand guitar to some truly beautiful instruments.

There is no doubt that music is at the core of who he is, but he will not be abandoning his day job and hitting the road for a world tour soon. He has formed a band with two friends who also share a passion for music alongside work and family commitments.

Bruce, who I am pleased to say is my husband, truly has no desire to be away from his family and on the road, but he loves to pull out his guitar and play at backyard barbecues anytime he gets a chance. His band has even been booked for some paying gigs, but that is not what drives any of the boys in the band. It is the music that drives them–they share a passion for performance, and it is hard to even imagine them without music in their lives.

They might have had to give up some "rock star dreams" along the way in order to find their real relationship with music, but there is no doubt that their passionate approach to music brings satisfaction for them and joy to those who hear it. This is the reality check of the MORE philosophy.

If you are realistic and you are honest with your expectations, you can live an exceptional life. If you are chasing a dream that really is inauthentic for you, it will only be a rat-race, and many of the opportunities of truly being present in your life might be lost. You can be true to yourself, contribute to others and follow your passion as well, but it does not usually work unless you are honest and real with yourself. You might not pursue guitar as it was never your passion, yet, you might choose to pursue your passion for puzzle solving instead, something that you love to do. That might be your route to success if it is something that you are truly talented at and you are willing to put significant time into it.

Honest Conversations ~The Forgotten Art of Conversation

In our politically correct society, we have forgotten how to have honest conversations with others, as well as with ourselves. In fact, we spend a lot of time talking in circles and not saying much of value, both in our self-conversations as well as in conversations with others. I am not saying that we should charge into a conversation like a bull in a china shop, but I am saying that we are spending far too much time thinking about how to say things in such a way that nobody will get upset or offended. We are far too busy protecting everybody's fragile ego, as well as our own. We are limiting our potential when we edit our internal conversations to the point where we do not deal with what is really going on in our lives.

The problem is that when discussing anything difficult or controversial, there is no way to actually say anything of value unless we are willing to take a risk. We can still be respectful to others, but if our goal is to avoid upsetting everybody then we have set a goal that cannot be accomplished, as somebody will eventually be offended in some manner or another. Again in a politically correct conversation people are aiming for a perfect conversation, rather than an honest conversation. When perfectionism gets in the way it works in opposition to the MORE philosophy and blocks the path to an exceptional experience. Trying to manage a life where we never offend another is a conflict-avoidant path, not a path to an exceptional life. Inevitably, a conflict avoidant approach is seldom satisfying or palatable to those around the person trying to avoid the difficult topic or situation.

That does not mean you should set out to be offensive in conversations. Respect and dignity are always important and should be at the core of every conversation. The following is a quick and effective way to evaluate if you are conducting yourself with integrity in a conversation.

The Five-Step Approach to a MORE Honest and Respectful Conversation

1. Ask yourself whether what you have to say is honest as far as you know. Is it based on something of substance and truth? Does it align with your values? If so then proceed to the second step.

2. If you have determined that you are speaking your truth, now ask yourself, "Is it necessary?" Does what you have to say have something of value to contribute to the conversation? Will it help you define something further or contribute to something outside yourself? If the answer is yes, proceed to the next step.

3. The third step is to evaluate whether you can say what you have to say in a manner that is kind and demonstrates respect for yourself and others. Is everyone's dignity still in place?

4. Take time to re-evaluate any uncertainty. If you are unsure of any of these steps, give yourself more time to think about them and do not rush. Sometimes when we percolate on thoughts, they brew into something exceptional. If you cannot answer a confident yes to the three steps above, re-evaluate. If you charge in without thought, it can take a significant amount of time and energy to clean up the conversation once the words have been spoken. Hurtful comments can completely derail a good conversation. Sometimes things are better left unsaid, but you do not have to abandon your thoughts if they do not meet the above criteria. Let the ideas continue to develop until they have met the first three criteria, and then those ideas have a much better chance at making a significant impact.

5. If you charged in and made a mess, forgive yourself but make it right as soon as possible. Apologize and take responsibility for any mess you made in a conversation, be brave and own it, and do not wait for the other person to apologize first. If you were careless or did not follow the above steps, do not be afraid to apologize. Let go of your pride and be a true leader. Lead the way towards an honest and respectful communication, and demonstrate that you can make mistakes and learn from them.

Again, the reality check is that you cannot control others, and that it is not your job to be responsible for how others process what you are saying. The reality is that it is your job to be responsible for what you are saying and you alone. There are as many perspectives of a situation as there are people in the world. If you are trying to tailor your conversation to each and every person and perspective out there you will end up saying nothing. You cannot please all of the people all of the time, and you cannot avoid displeasing people all of the time either.

There are times when it is most respectful to speak your truth, to say what you think and feel with dignity and respect by following the previous criteria, and then to allow others to respond and share their perspectives. This is called a conversation. There is respect, but there is no bullshit! It is like a tennis match that goes back and forth. The movement in the conversation occurs as you hit the ball to the other court and the other person returns it back to you. There is active participation in a conversation, and it is exciting when you feel the movement of ideas and thoughts going back and forth.

When you are both playing well, it is stimulating and it keeps you on your toes. This is also the way that good ideas become great. This is when the average can move to the exceptional.

If the other participant in the conversation is not playing fairly and not following the steps above for an honest and respectful conversation, then you might want to rethink whether you really want to be involved in that particular conversation. Your participation is your choice.

Conversations are meant to have vitality in them; and—yes—they may even be a little risky when people share important ideas. I believe in honest conversations and feel that these are sorely lacking in our politically correct world of communication. I am not saying that people should say anything they want or that it should be a communication "free for all," but I am saying that our concentration on making everything homogeneous and non-threatening can turn conversations into bland white bread with no substance or taste. There is not a lot of exciting tennis in politically correct conversations.

In the end, we will have many conversations in our lives, but when there is an emphasis on the correctness rather than on fair play, we have lost the true ability to create and stimulate, and to have an honest conversation. It is through honest conversations and the reality checks that these conversations bring forth, that we are able to apply the MORE philosophy to practice in our lives.

Questions for Contemplation

Do you fight mistakes, try to cover them up, or see them as opportunities?

Do you think you use excuses to cover up the real story?

Do you consider yourself a realist or a romantic?

Do you pay attention to the reality checks in your life?

Have you been able to "be anything you want in the world"?

Do you find honest conversations exciting, frightening, or both?

Do you feel you are speaking your truth in your conversations with others?

Do you think you generally follow the five-step approach to a respectful and honest conversation?

What is your blueprint of strengths and challenges?

How do you respond to feedback?

CHAPTER SEVEN

An Exceptional Life Will Hurt; Go with the Flow; Moving Through the Pain; Viewing Pain as a Gift.

"Accept that life hurts, especially an exceptional life....
and within the pain are the seeds of growth!"

Yes. Life hurts! There is no way around it. So much of our difficulties in life come from fighting against inevitable pain. Right from the moment of birth, we are fighting against the harsh reality and sensory overwhelm of this life. The more we step into this life, the more we will experience pain. Our existential pain and awareness of loss is part of the price of an exceptional life. This is the reality of the MORE philosophy. We cannot deny that pain is part of the human experience. To run from this pain and hide in distractions will limit our potential. To deny pain also limits our ability to be truly compassionate with others. We need our pain to develop and mature, and to bring our best selves to the opportunities that are presented along the way.

To illustrate how the fight against pain can cause great difficulties in life, yet also present an opportunity for transformation, I would like to share the stories of two highly sensitive and exceptional people who found the seeds of growth within their struggles.

Samuel

I first met Samuel when he was twelve. I have had the privilege of working with him as my client at different times throughout his life. A highly sensitive youth, he was struggling with the pain of peer issues at the private school he attended when I first met him. Being shy and self-conscious, he was overwhelmed by the other kids. He was very smart, but did not have many friends as he felt he did not fit in with his peers. He detested school, and much preferred to spend time with his "quirky" grandfather who taught him all about mechanics. He was a strong-willed boy and was increasingly agitated and refused to participate in the extracurricular activities his parents signed him up for.

It was soon clear to me that this boy was so sensitive, that he did not know how to handle the environment he was in. At times he could hardly tolerate the pain and sensory overwhelm he felt, so he tried to filter things out by detaching and pretending to not care.

He continued to struggle and once he entered into high school, he quickly dove into the world of drugs and alcohol. This was not a curious peek into the peer drug culture, wanting to try something new and exciting; this was a full on, over the deep end dive into addiction. It was not just his sensitivity he was struggling with, but rather a combination of many factors that ended up causing him a great deal of frustration and pain.

Within the first two months of high school, he experienced his first heartbreak when the girl he liked rejected him, then his sister was diagnosed with a serious illness and his much loved grandfather died suddenly. It was the "perfect storm" for Samuel and he was quickly lost in that storm.

He refused to attend school and was diagnosed with addiction issues and an anxiety disorder. His parents then sent him to an addiction treatment centre to deal with the alcohol and drug issue. He spent the next several months in treatment. It appeared that Samuel was doing well, so he returned home and went back to school.

He attempted to get back into the stream of life, but it was only a matter of weeks after his return that he once again dove head on into drugs and left home without telling anybody where he was. After going on a month-long binge, trying every possible drug he could lay his hands on, he not only exhausted his body and mind, but also his spirit, to the point where he could barely move. He returned home willingly, retreated and barely left his room, let alone the house.

I was deeply concerned for this boy and believed in his deep sensitivity and good heart, and his ability to overcome these challenges. This was not going to be a quick fix, but rather a long and difficult journey.

Part of the issue for Samuel was that his senses were so fine-tuned that the real world caused him too much physical pain and emotional overload. As a sensitive child he had always struggled with feelings of sadness and questions about the meaning of life. When the storm hit he had not built the inner strength yet to deal with the challenges around him. The combination of the death of a close attachment figure, his sister's serious illness, and his overwhelm with the rest of the world just made him want to escape everything.

He struggled with being able to screen out those around him and his overwhelming feelings of pain, so he tried to numb everything with drugs that were close and accessible to him. In order to screen out as much as possible he first used substances, but once he exhausted that avenue he retreated into his room and hid from the world and his pain. As is often the case, the fight against the pain was causing more problems than the pain. At sixteen, he was barely functioning in the real world, but he was still alive. And where there is life there is always the possibility for movement and opportunity.

Slowly, he came to understand himself and the gift of his sensitivity, and he began to build strength to match that sensitivity. He came to see that he had survived some very difficult times and earned his strength. He began to emerge in the world again, but this time he did so with a greater understanding of his vulnerabilities and how to take a step back when things overwhelmed him. He was ready to test himself again in the real world.

I am pleased to say that after a very difficult journey he is now in college and doing well in all aspects of his life. There is no doubt that those who care for him lost some sleep worrying about Samuel along the way, and as his therapist I can certainly attest to a few grey hairs that may have emerged from this case. It has been such a privilege to witness how he has maintained his sensitivity and built strength to balance this. He has become a great support to his sister and his parents. Samuel has also become involved in several organizations that assist others, and is in a steady relationship with a young woman who is also highly sensitive. He no longer uses drugs, and has even begun to volunteer with an organization that goes into schools and facilitates conversations with youth around drug and alcohol issues.

All in all, he came to the realization that he needed to learn how to deal with pain in order to take steps forward into an exceptional life. Samuel is an amazing example of someone who suffered great pain, who dove deep into despair, but has managed to come out of this a stronger, more compassionate person. He consistently contributes to others and is truly a good citizen of the world. He is also a reminder that we cannot judge somebody on their behaviour alone, and that the human spirit is resilient and can bounce back. At one point Samuel was so stuck, he had barely any movement in his life, but through applying the MORE Philosophy of step-by-step movement he was able to make slow but significant changes. Together we examined the opportunities that the MORE philosophy illuminated, and through paying attention to the realities in his life, Samuel reports that he is now living an exceptional life.

Pleasure and Pain

Inevitably, if we can accept emotional pain and trust our strength to deal with it, we can move toward an exceptional life. An exceptional life is seldom pretty and tidy, but with each challenge we overcome, we can build grace. It is rather ironic that the greatest challenge to maturity and exceptional living is no challenge. We need our pain to develop our character. In essence, to embrace our exceptional life we will need to accept the physical and emotional "growing pains" that come with maturation.   Physical pain can be so intense it completely dominates the moment it occupies, whereas emotional pain is often more difficult to understand and resolve. It is natural for our bodies to begin to heal and adapt in response to physical pain. We need to trust that it is also natural for us to heal and adapt through emotional pain.

Hurt feelings do not kill us, but it can take a long time to heal this type of pain if we avoid it. We get stuck when we ignore emotional pain and distract from it rather than moving through the pain. There will be times when life overwhelms each and every one of us and we will most likely feel victimized or burdened in some manner. But an important step to exceptional living is to trust our courage and our ability to persevere.

There is also pleasure in life to balance the pain, and if we are present in our lives we can better accept and enjoy the pleasure that is available as well. Both the pleasure and the pain provide opportunities to experience our lives. Of course most of us would rather choose pleasure, but often we do not get a choice in this. Opportunities both pleasurable and painful often just present themselves. When we trust ourselves and move through the experience, we make it to the other side. There are times when pleasure feels very fleeting, but if we allow pleasure to have its natural flow, it will move through us and we can actually experience the pleasure. If we are worrying about losing the pleasure, we have already lost it, as no feeling lasts forever. Neither physical sensation nor emotional feeling can sustain endlessly.

Step #9 ~ When Things Get Tough, Remember "I Can Handle It!"

When we are deep in grief or lost in pain we have to remind ourselves that this will not last forever. I have often told my clients, such as Samuel, that there will be a time when we look back on the difficulties. There is triumph when we get to the other side of a challenge and we remember how we overcame the pain and that we earned our strength and courage through the overcoming. But to do this we also have to trust that we can handle it.

When I work with people, especially children and youth, I remind them that the most important thing they can say when enduring pain is, "I can handle it." We should not lie to ourselves and say we feel no fear or anger or hurt. We need the reality check and we need to tell ourselves the truth, which is that, "I feel afraid," or "hurt," or "angry and I can handle it".

Anybody who has been through a physical trauma knows that they eventually came out the other end. It is likely that they came out battered and bruised and maybe even broken, but if they are there to tell the story, then they are still alive.

When we experience an emotional trauma we may feel as if we are going to die from the pain inside, but we do not. Nobody dies from an emotional pain. It may be heartbreaking, but the heart keeps beating. In truth, this pain is just part of the human experience, and we can overcome emotional trauma as well as physical trauma.

Martha

The struggle with emotional pain can be seen in the story of Martha. Let's dig into her life to understand this better. Martha is a lovely woman who exudes charm and charisma. People always enjoyed her dinner parties and wanted to be a part of her life. She seemed to have it together, but there were cracks in her life.

For example, the distance between herself and her husband was increasing; also, she did not feel close to her children now that they were teenagers. She felt something was wrong in her family but she did not know what it was or how to fix it.

When she checked her husband's text messages one day, her worst suspicions were confirmed–he was having an affair. She was furious. She had never felt such deep and searing pain. She had been married to this man for seventeen years and built her whole life around supporting him, helping him grow his business, and raising their children.

When she confronted him, he initially denied it, but eventually when faced with the evidence, he admitted the affair and told Martha that he was in love with the other woman and wanted a divorce. In the anger of that night things were said that dug them both deeper into their hurt. He left that night, but their story was not over. Their divorce was not going to be easy.

Prior to her husband's affair, both Martha and her husband had agreed that she would stay home with the kids, while he kept long hours at the office building the business. She did not want anybody else bringing up her children, so after the children were born , she decided not to return to her job. Her husband reassured her that he could make enough money for this to be a viable solution for the family. However all that blew up when she read those texts.

She was devastated that she had put so much of her life on hold for her family, and she felt that she had done this at the urging of her husband. Now she was left alone and without current skills, her dreams were shattered. And, rather than apologize and beg for forgiveness, her husband informed her he wanted to move out and that he was in love with somebody else.

Feeling abandoned and betrayed by her husband, Martha turned that pain into anger and was determined that he was going to pay for what he had done. She told herself that she needed to protect herself and the kids. She was not going to let him give away everything they had worked for to some horrible woman who had an affair with a married man with children. She retained the toughest lawyer she could find and readied herself for battle, and instructed her lawyer to get every penny he could for her and the children.

At first, Martha turned to her friends and family and told them of the betrayal, insisting they be on her side. Then she started to confide in her children about the end of the relationship and the legal issues, justifying her inclusion of the children in the legal issues by telling herself that they needed to know the truth. She did not want the children to spend time with their father because she felt he had left the family, and if they spent time with him it would be sending the message that what he did was okay. Then, she told the neighbourhood and all the parents at the school. Then, she told the people who worked in their family business. Then, she told anybody who would listen.

Initially, Martha received support and caring from those around her, but soon people were not answering her calls and her social invitations decreased. Her children also increasingly avoided her and their home. Her daughter specifically became sullen and quiet, while her son was never home anymore; and when he was home, all he did was bark orders and insults at her, just like his father used to do. On the whole, Martha was feeling alone, depressed, frightened, scared and in a lot of pain.

In life, we can get ourselves stuck in pain. The more people try to avoid pain, the more they find themselves right in the middle of a swirling vortex of the emotions they are trying to deny. As I assist families through divorce and separation in my counselling practice, I see many people devastated by the end of their relationship, but still spinning around on perceived hurts and old violations long past the end of the marriage.

This was Martha. Her pain was real, and her feelings were valid, but she was beginning to spin on her pain rather than truly grieve the relationship. It was easier to be angry and plan revenge, rather than to feel the grief. Ultimately, her anger was turning to bitterness and even her children were beginning to avoid her, as she was so highly focused on the conflict and how their father had betrayed them all. There was so much sadness in this family—they were all heading in opposite directions, each still being consumed by pain, but nobody moving through it.

When we accept our lives and the pain that comes with it, we can start to find dignity and grace.

People wanted to support and care for Martha, but they could not stay connected to her energy once she became bitter and self-focused. She forgot to ask other people how they were doing and what was new in their lives. She stopped being curious. She forgot that she could "handle it."

Others stopped telling her about their own lives as everything seemed insignificant compared to hers, and they started to avoid her, as the only thing she wanted to talk about was the divorce. In fact, her own children did not feel safe to share their feelings with her; they worried this would become evidence against their father in some legal battle. She was losing them as well. She was not creating a safe place for the children to process their feelings of hurt, anger, and loss. Yet she justified her continued remarks about their father as protecting the children in some way.

When we notice that others are withdrawing from us, it is an opportunity for a reality check and an opportunity to make some changes. We are in charge of our perceptions and how we deal with the reality checks that life provides.

In this case, Martha had a choice: she could look at her increasing isolation and ask herself why people were not returning her calls, or she could see people withdrawing from her as a reason to feel even more let down and betrayed by the world. As long as Martha chose to see herself as a victim, her life was a life without movement, a life that was spinning on itself and was missing the points of connection that were right there in front of her. If she continued to ignore the reality checks and refused to feel the grief, she could not move toward the exceptional life that was possible for her. Her life was becoming smaller and smaller. Overall, if she could find the grace and dignity to lead her children through this difficult time, she could model strength, courage, and resiliency to them.

Eventually, Martha did start to pay attention to the reality checks and realized she needed to make some changes. She sought counselling and came to accept her pain, and understood she could "handle it" and that she would survive this difficult time in her life. The pain of her marital breakdown would not kill her; in fact, it would actually be the opportunity for her to uncover hidden strengths she did not even know she had. She had done nothing "wrong" and still her vision had failed. There are times that no matter how well intentioned the vision and goal, things still fail and fall apart.

Once she began to truly grieve the loss in a safe space with a skilled therapist, she was able to move through the pain and accept the changes that occurred. To make movement forward we need to feel our pain, and accept the futility of a situation. These tears of futility can be "gut wrenching", but there is release and movement after we have accepted a loss and our lack of ability to control things in life. In fact, there is often almost a feeling of elation after we have truly accepted and felt our pain. Now there is room for the other emotions to emerge.

Martha moved through her grief and then she began to see that she had said too much to her children and they needed to have a significant relationship with their father. She also came to understand that although he had disappointed and betrayed her, he was a good father and the children benefitted from their time with him. She began to see that she had compromised too much to hold onto her vision of one family together, and that she had been denying reality for some time.

When she really looked at it and began to have an honest conversation with herself, she realized that her marriage had been disconnected for some time: it had been a long time since they had talked about anything other than the kids and the business. She also realized she had missed the warning signals, as well as some opportunities to connect with her husband in the past. She did not support his choices and she was deeply sad that their marriage ended with his affair, but she began to adapt.

She reconnected with friends and began going out socially again. She stopped discussing her hurt feelings about the divorce with her children. She changed lawyers and started working collaboratively with her husband and his lawyer to form a separation agreement that preserved the dignity and financial resources of the family. Martha attended co-parenting counselling with her husband, where they learned how to communicate in a new way and discussed how to keep the needs of the children a priority in the process. She apologized to her children for involving them in the adult issues, and for interfering in their relationship with their father. She even shared some of her grief with her husband and accepted his apology. In turn, she realized that he was not proud of his actions or how things ended.

Eventually, Martha even began dating again, and she found that she was a much more adaptive person who no longer felt she had to be the "Martha Stewart" of the neighbourhood. Her children also adapted when she moved on, and no longer felt torn between their parents. Once Martha truly accepted her grief and cried her tears of loss, she began to move the pain; and as the pain moved, new opportunities emerged.

Martha is now in a new relationship with another man who has also been through a divorce. They are still figuring things out as they go and trying to fit all the different pieces of their lives together, but they are open and honest with each other about the joys and the struggles.

After many honest conversations and the acceptance of her pain, Martha reports that she is living an exceptional life. She has great relationships with her teenage children and a civil and functional relationship with her ex-husband. She has re-entered the workforce and is enjoying her job. She feels more at ease and authentic than she ever has in her life.

People used to feel overwhelmed by her parties, as they were so "perfect," but things have changed with Martha—dinner at her house is more relaxed and enjoyable than ever, as she is not quite so concerned about having everything just right. She is not a victim of her ex-husband, her friends, her children, or anybody else, and she is certainly not a victim of her life anymore. She understands pain and listens well when others speak of their losses, as she can truly empathize with them. She now enjoys the reality of her life much more than the vision she held onto for so long. She is using the four principles of MORE to be realistic and to pursue the new opportunities that emerge. All in all, she is an exceptional friend, mother, and partner, and she still throws a great dinner party!

Chapter 7

Questions for Contemplation

How do you handle physical pain?

How do you handle emotional pain?

Have you ever felt so overwhelmed by emotional pain that you felt you could not function?

Have you been stuck in emotional pain?

Do you feel you can "handle it" when you face a challenge?

Do you believe you can adapt?

Do you see your strength and resiliency?

Can you look back at a difficult time and see that it is now in the past?

Can you think of a time you took adversity and moved it to opportunity?

CHAPTER EIGHT

Duality; Working toward Authenticity; The Battle between External and Internal Reality; The Light and Dark in Each of Us; The Battle Between "Good" and "Evil" Within.

"Our greatest gift is also our greatest challenge; this is the double-edged sword of life."

We have discussed several principles of an exceptional life. It is my hope that the principles explored in this book will assist you in reaching a higher level of self-honesty and self-awareness. In order to live an exceptional life, we need to have a sense of our external and internal identities. To be able to make conscious choices and be responsible for the consequences and benefits of our choices, we need to be honest with ourselves about our own complex natures and the battle between "good" and "evil" within. Each person has a capacity for construction and destruction; as we travel the road of life we will experiment with both sides of our nature.

Part of an honest conversation is to admit that the light and dark exist in every one of us! Jungian Psychology often refers to this contrast as "The Shadow" and the less aware we are of our dark side, the bigger the shadow we cast. It is through conscious movement and honesty we can become aware of our dark side. It is my belief that this side is not the "bad" side of us, but rather it is the side that is complex, creative, and exciting. This excitement can have an element of danger, but that does not mean it has to be destructive. It is the choice we make that can determine whether our dark side will be either destructive or constructive.

The duality of the human experience has been illustrated throughout history and in different cultures. The Tao (yin and yang) is an example of this. The yin is often characterized as the sensitive and nurturing side of our nature and the yang as the strong and active side of us. The yin and yang symbol is illustrated by a simple and beautiful representation of white and black semi-circles reaching into each other—two halves making a whole. This is a very simple and effective illustration of a deeper truth. Neither side is more valuable than the other. One without the other is incomplete, and together they make a whole. This is symbolic of human nature—to achieve a complete and exceptional life we need to understand both sides of our nature.

Duality appears everywhere, in many ways, and is illustrated in almost all religions and cultural stories in some manner. In Western cultures and religion, we have the story of God and the Devil. The Devil is often seen in dark and dramatic colors surrounded by blackness and fire, while God is dressed in white and illuminated by light. This can be seen as good and evil, the hero and the villain, or it can just be seen as two halves that need each other in order to make the whole. If we dig a little deeper into these stories, we can see the actual life lessons that are there for all to learn. If we connect the dots and decipher the metaphors in cultural and religious stories, there is much there that connects humanity, allowing us the opportunity to appreciate the unique and interesting differences that the world has to offer.

Duel of Duality

Many of the great cultural and religious stories feature some sort of struggle regarding duality. As stated earlier, there really is no good story without a problem. The struggle for balance between the dark and the light can create some pretty interesting problems, and thus some pretty interesting stories. Most stories seem to fall into a few dominant and repetitive themes. One of these categories is the "duel of duality." In other words, the battle is between good and bad, the hero and the villain. This struggle can be conveyed externally through the different characters or it can be conveyed through the main characters' struggle with some sort of choice within. Often the story will encompass both internal and external struggles, which parallel each other.

A recent and hugely successful example of this theme was the Harry Potter series. Readers witnessed Harry struggle with his internal powers, as well as his external struggle with the evil Lord Voldemort. In many ways, it is a simple story that has been told thousands of times, but we never seem to tire of this theme as it represents a deep and universal human challenge. Overall, the struggle between good and evil, light and dark is at the core of human experience.

Although we enjoy the excitement of the battle, in the end we love it when the "good" side wins. However, this is never a simple journey as it requires courage and awareness from the main character of the story, as well as a choice regarding how to use power. There is often risk, pain, and sacrifice in the hero's journey. I believe we are all the lead characters in our own story, and just as Harry struggled with power both inside and outside of himself, we also have our own problems to overcome and our own balance to achieve.

In order to obtain balance we need both our yin and yang. We need our dark and our light sides to balance. We similarly need Harry Potter and Voldemort in order to have a good story. It is the problems and the struggles that make humans truly interesting. Ultimately, our greatest strength is also our greatest weakness and that is the double-edged sword we wield.

Step #10 ~ Learn How to Wield Your Double-Edged Sword

In many hero stories, the hero has a sword; a sword that has both edges sharpened is a powerful tool. This image of the double-edged sword helps symbolize the internal and external struggle we have with both the light and the dark side of our selves, as well as how our greatest strengths and vulnerabilities are usually one and the same. Life would be static and boring if we were perfectly balanced and did not need to adapt to overcome challenges, as a sword would be of little use were it not designed with an edge. Both halves of the double-edged sword are always connected and we minimize its usefulness if we deny either edge.

An example of strength and vulnerability co-existing together is found in studying what it takes to be a good therapist. There is no doubt that a truly effective therapist will need to have well developed compassion, kindness and the ability to encourage others. But much like anyone with high sensitivity and compassion, a person who offers these gifts to others can end up suffering from compassion fatigue and a feeling of overwhelming responsibility. Leadership is another commonly seen area where the double edge is visible. Many effective leaders I have spoken with describe the struggle they have between the drive to contribute to others and the personal desire for power and significance. To live a conscious and real life through the MORE philosophy, one has to become aware that our motivation and characteristics are like a double-edged sword. We are neither "good" nor "bad," but rather complex people with many motivations that could be interpreted in many different ways. Our greatest strengths and weaknesses will always continue to co-exist together; it is only our level of awareness that we can change.

Once we become aware of this, however, we can use our double-edged sword within to access our greatest assets. I encourage you to remain aware of what is on the other side of the sword, so that you can make well-informed decisions that lead to an exceptional life. In turn, this is the honest conversation you can have with yourself, and it is my hope that by sharing your honest conversation, you may even inspire others to do so as well.

If we refuse to risk losing face and only want to look "pretty" or "nice," then we will not be able to access the true power within. The exceptional life is one that is a double-edged sword, but this sword can be used to build and illuminate or it can carry a power to destroy. If we never pick up the sword out of fear of our own power, we might never have to face our fears, and thus we risk or gain nothing. But is this the life you want? No risk, no accountability, no passion? To be a great swordsman, one has to know their instrument, understand what it is made of and not be afraid to practice using it.

Awareness

I believe it is a blessing and a curse that our greatest strengths are also our greatest weaknesses, but the knowledge of this can keep us accountable, as well as exceptional. If we are compassionate, we may worry too much. If we are interested in leadership, we might struggle with power. If we are sensitive, we might be overwhelmed. If we have a good sense of humour, we might minimize our pain. If we are easily forgiving, we may struggle with boundaries. If we are highly aware, we may have trouble filtering, and if we have rigid boundaries we might alienate others.

Whatever the weakness, there is a strength on the other side of the sword. Conversely, whatever the strength, there is a vulnerability on the other side. It is not as simple as "good" or "bad"—it is about awareness and how you choose to wield your sword.

Some never pick up the sword out of fear; they live unfulfilled lives. Some deny that it is a sword and live an unaware life. Some use the sword to destroy and live a selfish life, whereas others have the courage to pick up the sword, aware of its strengths and flaws, and use it in a way that can benefit others.

We all have different strengths and assets and it is up to each of us to test ourselves and discover what these are—then we can choose how to channel our strengths. It is my belief that all humans have a double-edged sword within, and the more aware and honest we are about it, the more informed and accountable we will be for our choices. Once we understand that duality is natural, and that we do not have to deny one side of our nature, we can then understand that true freedom comes when we accept who we are. Once we have accepted all sides of ourselves, we can then manage and direct our motivations.

Step #11 ~ Contribute to Others

Accountability

The reality of the MORE philosophy keeps us accountable and moves us toward constructive choices. Without reality checks, there is no conscious accountability to our practice and choices. If I work very hard to be truthful to myself about my motivations, I am then able to make decisions that will be both constructive to me and others.

Sometimes, truly constructive decisions require a sacrifice, or a loss of something that is difficult for us to let go of. The loss is usually associated with the selfish part of us that was simply focusing on what we wanted (such as to retain ego and pride). I have come to understand that only thinking of what I want keeps me small, and that thinking of ways to be of service to others leads me to the exceptional life. To paraphrase an old Buddhist saying, "The greatest joy in life comes from giving and doing for another, whereas the greatest pain in life comes from doing or thinking just of oneself."

I believe this to be true—if I am honest then I can see that my greatest joys have been when I have been of service to others, and my greatest pain has come when I was only thinking of myself. When we only feel sorry for ourselves and concentrate on how others have hurt us, then we are being self-centred. When we are grabbing at whatever we want regardless of others, we are also being selfish. We all feel sorry for ourselves sometimes; this is natural. But if we allow ourselves to spend too much time wallowing in our sorrow; we end up wasting our time and avoiding the real work that needs to be done.

Yet, I have also come to understand that my greatest learning and growth have come when my ego and pride have been humbled. Sometimes, the best thing is to "lose face" in order to see ourselves better.

A long time ago I committed to the path of being a lifelong learner. At that time, I did not realize what that commitment would entail; I only knew I was curious and I would find joy in learning. I was already moving toward the exceptional life that is possible through MORE.

Conversely, there is not just joy in learning; there is also something incredibly humbling in our most significant life lessons. If you want to keep learning be prepared to take chances, but also be prepared to be humbled and to let go of your pride. Once we are aware of our ego we can keep it in check and channel that power toward something bigger than just our self.

Each of us will have the duel of duality in our story somewhere. This is an important MORE Philosophy life lesson—by being honest with ourselves, by admitting and understanding our flaws as well as our powers, we can make a choice to participate in the world and channel our powers constructively. We may have to make some sacrifices along the way, but we will find ourselves in a great, purposeful story surrounded by real connections with others—an exceptional life that can go to eleven. If we choose to ignore these lessons, and simply remain a character that makes selfish decisions, life may ultimately feel lonely, empty, and without purpose. If we live life in this selfish way, we become the antithesis of a hero, and our path to the exceptional life is clouded and out of reach.

Nevertheless, we are all pulled toward some selfish decisions, and it is human nature to experiment with our duality and the choices we are presented with. However, if you find yourself surrounded by the trappings of success, feeling empty, and dissatisfied, then beware—your sword may not be balanced! It is then time to use your courage: change the road you are on and get ready for some sacrifices. You might actually get to know yourself better and come to understand your authentic self through these sacrifices.

It is true that it can be painful to sacrifice, but if we do not learn how to give without loss, then we choose a primarily selfish path, and in the long run we will live a much smaller and more isolated life. We will not touch as many lives and our legacy will be limited. Our courage will not be tested and we will hold on tightly to the things we are not willing to sacrifice. We will use our sword only to protect ourselves, rather than our family, our community, or our world. We might find ourselves just grasping onto things rather than to people.

An exceptional life might be filled with a bit of chaos, and some obstacles to overcome, but it will also be filled with connection and closeness. Balance is part of an exceptional life. We need to accept that each of us has a "dark" side and a "light" side. We will struggle with choosing between the motivation to contribute and the desire to take for ourselves, but as we experience the joy that comes with contribution and service to others we will move toward a more fulfilled and purposeful life. It is in these moments that we take that step #1 of the MORE philosophy where we turn it up to an eleven. When we, as well as others, feel our passion and purpose, we are living vibrant and exciting lives.

Self-Inventory about Your Sword

What is a quality you are proud of, or see as a positive quality?

What is the characteristic on the other side, the cost or dark side of that quality?

Can you think of a time you used the dark side of your sword?

When you used the dark side were you thinking of yourself or others?

How did this make you feel?

Can you think of a time you used the light side of the sword?

When you used the light side of the sword were you thinking of yourself or others?

How did that make you feel?

What are you afraid to sacrifice?

What do you give most freely?

Do you agree or disagree that our greatest joy comes through contribution and our greatest pain comes when we think only of ourselves?

How do you contribute to others, and when do you feel you are of service?

Think of one thing you can do for a friend, for your family, for your community, and for the greater good.

CHAPTER NINE

An Exceptional Life Harmonizes the Individual Personality to Achieve a Balanced Life.

"We need our armour, we need our soft hearts, and we need to learn how and when to use these aspects of ourselves."

Balance is one of the many ingredients that will assist you in creating an exceptional life. Although an exceptional life has moments of challenge and moments of joy, it also has a certain balance to it. I do not mean balance as in a flat line, but more in a see-saw kind of way. Life is a bit of a teeter totter, in which we need to be able to draw on different aspects of our personality and identity.

As we saw in Chapter Eight, we need to understand and balance the different sides of our nature, and we also need to be able to pull on our different internal resources depending on the external situation we are in. This requires a balance of identity as well as of nature.

This chapter will illustrate and help you understand the different personality characteristics that you need to live your balanced life.

There has been much attention lately on life-work balance. Many people are feeling overwhelmed and are trying to figure out how to balance all the responsibilities, pressures, and expectations in life. Although we will spend some time on this in Chapter Ten, in this chapter, I want to describe the psychological balance that we need within, before we discuss the balance needed in the world outside. Once we understand this internal balance, the external balance is much easier to achieve.

The Teeter Totter

In order to balance something, we need to distribute weight on both ends of a level surface. There is no better illustration of this than a teeter totter at a playground. Imagine a teeter totter: when only one end is weighted, there is no balance. As a child, I used to love to go to the playground, and my friends and I would go up and down on the teeter totter for hours. Finding the rhythm was both a joy and a challenge. It sure wasn't any fun being all by yourself on a teeter totter –this was an activity that required both sides to be engaged in order to achieve any satisfaction. In the end, balance on any teeter totter requires two people. Likewise, we need to be able to access both sides of our identity to find psychological balance.

As in any exhilarating activity or adventure story, the danger is also part of the fun. And even on something as simple as a teeter totter, the hint of physical danger is part of the allure. The fact that you might fall off, be bumped, or lose your balance adds a bit of spice to a simple activity. It is the same with our psycho-logical balance: there will be times we are thrown off or lose our balance, and these times make for some interesting experiences. A perfect balance is not what we are seeking. Although occasion-ally, just like two people on a teeter totter, we might achieve a magical moment of alignment. On the teeter totter, as in life, we can experience those moments of suspension as beautiful feelings of weightlessness. Then, the moment is lost and the movement returns and we resume our rhythm. We are not meant to stay in suspension even if it is a magical moment. Instead, we are meant to enjoy the moment and have plenty of movement on either side!

When we examine the mechanics of balance, we understand that when the weights are similar there will be some sort of stability. Things may weigh a little more on one side, but we can still manage to create rhythm and balance for the whole. It is seldom that we experience pure alignment as there is no movement there, but we can create balance through adjusting variables, just like on a teeter totter when we could move forward and back in order to achieve balance.

Psychological Balance

Humans seek and need balance in both a physical and psychological manner. Just like the physical balance two children seek on a teeter totter, we also need balance between the psychological parts of ourselves. If we look at the duality of our physical self, we see that it is much easier to balance in this world when we have two legs and two arms. To disrupt, break, or lose one of our limbs puts us out of balance. It takes a great deal of work and adjustment to find a new balance once a limb is injured or lost.

It is the same with our psychological self. We need to find a balance between the limbs of our psychological self, and if there is a disruption or disturbance, we might need to adjust to find our psychological balance. So what are the two sides that need to be balanced? On one side we have our emotional and intuitive self, and on the other side we have our rational and logical self. Both these sides of our nature are required for a balanced and exceptional life.

Step #12 ~ Know Which Side of Yourself to Pull on at the Right Time

Each of our psychological sides has a purpose and is needed for optimal functioning. This does not mean that one must be perfectly balanced at all times, but rather it means that in order to lead an exceptional life the principle of balance is needed. The MORE philosophy and the awareness of our internal duality will bring us opportunity and chances for success. Not only do we need both aspects of ourselves, but one of the important steps to living an exceptional life is knowing what part of the self to pull on at the right moment. Balance is not about equality, but rather about learning how and when to access different aspects of the self. If our identity is developed both logically and emotionally, we have more resources. Even if we are overdeveloped in one area and underdeveloped in the other, we can still find a psychological balance, if we adjust ourselves.

This is much like my experience on the teeter totter with my friends. I was often larger than my friends but I would shift my weight and lean forward in order to find that balance. Sometimes we have to shift and lean forwards when it comes to our personality as well.

This same principle applies to the balance between our conscious-rational self and our intuitive-emotional self. We do not need to have perfect distribution of weight on each side in order to have balance. If we are aware of ourselves, and are able to adjust and adapt as needed, we will be able to pull on the most useful resources when the time is needed.

We might need to rethink the value we place on either our emotions or our intellect. Neither side of the self is more important than the other. For simplicity's sake, imagine your rational logical self as located in your mind and your head, and your emotional-intuitive self as located in your chest and your heart. It is much like the teeter totter we were discussing earlier with the fulcrum of our strength and resiliency in the middle distributing the weight; but this system lives within us. It is active and moving at all times. When we are able to learn how to manage it, we can find the balance we need in order to best respond to our lives.

You may find that you primarily identify with one side of your identity. Some people might be very comfortable in their logic and reason and steer away from their emotions; others may feel that emotions are much more important than anything else. In fact, both are necessary. Again, the emotional and rational are needed to make the whole.

Chapter 9

The Rational Self

Let's first focus on the "Rational Conscious Self." I am going to introduce you to three members of the rational team that all work together. It might help to imagine this team managing a kingdom, the kingdom of the rational self. There is the Guard, the Informant, and the Analyst. First we will explore the Guard.

The Rational Self ~ The Guard

This is our suit of armour and the protection we build around our self; it is the filter and shield we use between ourselves and the rest of the world. This is the side of us that is self-protective, and its main job is to ensure our safety. There is nothing wrong with protecting yourself in this world—in fact it is essential. Humans are born vulnerable and need to develop some self-protection in order to survive. We do need a shield to protect us from the bows and arrows of this world. There are many times when it is appropriate to respond to the world in a guarded and cautious manner.

In order to live an exceptional life, you need to have a Guard who stays alert and pays attention. Nevertheless, as on any team, if one person becomes too zealous, he/she can take over the agenda and lose sight of the desired team outcome. As explored in Chapter Two, we generally do not experience life-threatening dangers on a daily basis anymore, but we do experience a sense of emotional vulnerability. An effective Guard protects our vulnerable self. Like any good Guard, it needs to manage the defence step-by-step and know when to take down the fortifications in order to let in those who are welcome. A healthy Guard checks that the person entering the fortress has appropriate papers and is safe to let in. Just like a fortress still needs supplies, visitors and news from the outside world to make it a vibrant and functioning community, a person needs to connect with the outside world in order to be healthy and fulfilled.

However, if we give the Guard free reign, he could guard us from living an exceptional life. Sometimes our Guard overreacts to the threat of emotional pain, and thinks it has to build an even thicker, impenetrable fortress. The fortress is secured, and weapons are readied. The Guard might begin to react as if under siege. If we perceive a threat or attack, and the Guard feels we cannot handle the threat, the weapons are activated. We may need to remind our Guard that we "can handle it." If we let the Guard run the kingdom, we probably have things ass-backward again. An over-activated Guard may become aggressive and attack first in order to get the advantage and cover up any vulnerability.

We all know people who have highly activated Guards who seem to be in control of the kingdom, and some of us may even recognize this about ourselves. We perceive a threat of some sort, so we park all the emotions in a safe place and bring out the cold and razor-sharp logic. We can use this logic and reason to cut down others and disable them before they are able to harm us in any way. We reject the other before we can be rejected. We devalue the other before we can be devalued.

The following is a good example of how becoming too guarded can actually get in the way of the best things in life.

Bob and Sophia

This reminds me of a couple who attended counselling with me. Bob was a highly intelligent, successful man in his mid-forties who ran a large multinational company. He was personable, cultured, and admired, but he was also highly guarded and did not have many real friends. He had constructed a life in which very little could hurt him and he was not deeply attached to those around him. A lot was expected of him in his highly competitive business world and he often had to make quick and cut-throat decisions that impacted a lot of people. It did not pay off for him to be vulnerable in front of his competitors or his staff.

His work success was not mirrored in his family life. He had two failed marriages and was currently dating Sophia, a woman he was considering marrying, but he felt unsure about the situation.

Bob thought highly of Sophia, as he admired her success in business and felt she was a good match for him in many ways. She was younger than him and wanted marriage and children. He was concerned that if he did not marry Sophia, she would leave. As she was attractive, intelligent, and accomplished—he did not want to lose her.

Nevertheless, he was not sure if it was the right move to marry her. He already had children with his first two wives and paid a considerable amount of money in child and spousal support. He felt overwhelmed with commitments already, and only saw his children twice a month as he was very busy with his job and often travelled for his work. He did not think he wanted more children, but he knew Sophia did. Bob was not a highly engaged father and felt he was doing his best for his children by sending them to private schools and taking them on at least one expensive yearly holiday.

Although he was dating a beautiful woman and lived in a beautiful home, Bob indicated that he did not feel happy with the way things were in his life. He was concerned about getting married for a third time and did not want it to end in another divorce.

Sophia and Bob attended couples counselling together to explore the issues that had come up in their relationship. Sophia reported that she thought Bob was charming and great company, but often found him to be critical of her. She indicated that he would use his humour in a way that sometimes demeaned her. When she addressed him on this, he always told her that she had no sense of humour. She felt she loved him, but she understood that there were already some problems in the relationship and was starting to rethink things and question whether Bob was the right man for her.

They attended couples counselling after a few big arguments in which Sophia threatened to break off the relationship. Bob would say cold and cutting things during these arguments, and

Sophia found herself getting more reactive and emotional in order to just get an emotional response out of him.

In essence, Bob had a highly activated Guard who did not trust that Bob could "handle it," so the Guard kept him behind high walls and everyone else at a distance. The Guard would also make sure it stayed in control, and would use its intellect as a weapon when someone who might make Bob vulnerable approached too near. Both his ex-wives described him as cold and uncaring. His children wanted his approval, and were never sure if they were getting it or not. He did not yell at them or discipline them, but he was seldom engaged with his children and they worried that they were unimportant to him.

As Bob and Sophia progressed in their counselling Bob learned how to pull back his defences and open himself up to having a real relationship, which included risks and vulnerabilities. He came to accept that there would be pain in his relationships, and that it would not destroy him. Bob closely examined the costs of living life so guarded and committed to making some significant changes. Sophia learned to manage her reactions better and give Bob space to process things when he got overwhelmed or defensive.

They did eventually get married after they had worked through these challenges and they have a young child today. Bob reported that the work he did in counselling actually helped him have a much closer relationship to all his children, and a more constructive relationship with his ex-wives. He even found that by becoming more authentic and less fearful of exposure he was better at his work and did not feel consumed with the need to prove and protect himself. He felt his creative energy was at an all-time high and his business was actually doing better than ever. Sophia reports that Bob is a caring husband and a loving father and she feels they now have the tools to work through issues as they emerge.

It might have taken Bob a while to learn some of these life lessons, and there is no doubt that his lessons cost him both financially and relationally, but he did eventually work through his defences. Bob was able to apply the principles of the MORE philosophy and now reports that he is fully engaged in his exceptional life and more satisfied than he has ever been.

Conflict

Many of us may recognize some of these traits. We might have found ourselves in an argument with someone else, even someone we care for very deeply, and our dominant Guard might have taken over. We might find ourselves saying hard, cold, and cutting things to the person we are having a conflict with. This does not usually make the relationship better or resolve the argument. The Guard is not trying to resolve the issue; rather, its job is to protect the vulnerable self.

When one person who is in a conflict becomes detached and dispassionate, a dynamic is often created in which the other person in the conflict becomes more emotional in order to get a reaction. This was the case with Sophia: the more logical Bob became, the more emotional she became.

Even though this emotional-rational dyad is a clumsy attempt at balance, it just digs the conflict deeper. Who is right and who is wrong does not really matter, as the end result is usually one person experiencing a lonely sense of superior isolation and the other feeling frustrated, unheard and unknown. This way of dealing with conflict just separates us further from each other. This might "win" you the argument but it will not achieve closeness and connection with another.

The Rational Self ~ The Informant

The Rational Self is not always concentrating on building fortresses and wielding weapons; it is also intent on gathering information. Knowledge is power, and in order to live an exceptional life, we need to be able to pay attention to the world we are in. This is part of the reality check of the MORE philosophy. The next member of our rational team is called "The Informant." This is the spy within.

The Informant works very closely with the Guard, but plays a different role. The Informant gathers information. Is there a threat here? Is there a potential vehicle to achieve my goal? What are the characteristics of the person I am talking to right now? The Informant can be in full swing at a cocktail party, a board meeting, or in our most intimate relationships and even the quietest of moments.

We need to understand the environment around us in order to make well-informed decisions. The Informant is particularly helpful in a new situation, but never stops collecting information no matter the environment. There are many ways to gather information and the Informant can be pleasant, friendly and a great conversationalist as well as quiet and observational. The Informant can also be very secretive and covert. If we feel that information is difficult to gather or is being withheld, the spy is sent out to assess if there is some sort of threat lurking around the corner with the potential for emotional hurt. If we feel that something is wrong in one of our close relationships, the Informant will often go looking for clues and proof: much like Martha who felt something was "off" and went searching through her husband's text messages. Again, if the threat is confirmed, the Guard may come out and take over. If no immediate threat is perceived, the Guard retreats and the Informant continues to listen and learn.

Step #13 ~ Stay Curious

Curiosity

The Informant is also the great student within us. Our rational mind loves new information and a healthy Informant is highly curious. Curiosity itself is not aimed at self-protection, but rather at self-growth and innovation. New information is interesting and it builds our awareness and participation in the world around us. I believe that in order to have an exceptional life, we need to stay curious. We need to ask questions about the things we do not know; we need to consider different opinions and thoughts; and we need to wonder about the people around us. We do not have to have all the answers; rather we need to ask the questions. Curiosity will keep us engaged in our life and connected to others around us. This curiosity extends to learning about new people and new experiences. By allowing our curiosity to drive us deeper into our present interests and experiences, it also digs us deeper into our relationships.

People are endlessly interesting if you allow them to be so. Allow people a space to talk and express themselves. We all want to know and be known. A life with balance has the ability to hold onto the self and also to listen to others. We become boring to others if we just try to fill the space up with ourselves and stop being curious. Remember what happened to Martha after her marital separation? She lost her curiosity and then people started avoiding her as they did not feel she was interested in them any longer. You do not have to agree with everyone else, and you are always allowed to have your own opinion and thoughts, but remain open minded to the experience of another person.

Curiosity is a gift of the human mind, and it supplies endless entertainment for us. Inevitably, without curiosity there is no creativity, and when we allow ourselves curiosity our Rational Self, like a child in a playground, enjoys all the different opportunities to experience and learn more. Truly innovative ideas come from this place. When we become curious about something and open ourselves to gathering information about it, we can then weave together the different information and eventually a new and original thought may arise within us. Sometimes these thoughts and ideas are things we bring forth to the world around us, and we might even be able to contribute something that can make an impact and be of value to others.

The Rational Self ~ The Analyst

Once the Informant or "spy within" has gathered the information, it is then analyzed. Our rational brain is highly analytical, organizing and reviewing the information in a way that will illuminate a path toward a goal. This third member of the team is the "Analyst," and this part of our rational mind is very helpful when planning and organizing. To avoid chaos and run a well-managed life we need the Analyst to assist us in sorting and compartmentalizing the information, keeping what is important and letting go of what is unimportant. We collect vast amounts of information every day of our lives and we need a way of organizing it.

The Analyst will see patterns and categories and assist us in making sense of all the input. If we want to achieve our goals, we need our Analyst. The movement toward the successful completion of a goal goes hand-in-hand with our analytical mind. This is not an enemy nor a part of us to be overcome, but rather an effective vehicle toward living an exceptional life. We cannot "wing it" all the time and we need a plan to bring our goals to fruition. This is part of the movement of the MORE philosophy. One of the strong messages coming from brain science these days is that to keep our brains healthy, we need to keep learning new things. The rational mind loves learning new things, and is open to a flow of new information.

To review, the Analyst is the one inside the tower weaving a tapestry and helping put all the information into a coherent picture that has a pattern and a purpose. Our Informant leaves the castle to gather information, and our Guard is there to protect and manage the gates.

To illustrate the rational team in action, think about any truly great presentation you have either delivered or attended. All members of the team are needed. If a person is giving a presentation, the Guard needs to tuck away the emotions so the person is not vulnerable to seeking approval or fearing rejection. Although it is natural to feel anxious or excited, a powerful presenter does not want their own emotions to distract from the message at hand. The Informant will scan for vital information like the size of the room, how many people are in the room, and what technical support is needed. An effective speaker will keep taking in information and will continue to assess throughout the presentation, evaluating the level of interest from the crowd and determining whether adjustments are needed if the crowd seems to be losing interest. The Analyst keeps the delivery of information on task in order to achieve the best outcome. This rational conscious mind is needed to create an exceptional presentation, just like the rational conscious mind is needed to create an exceptional life.

The rational mind is also needed at home. For example, if my children are misbehaving I will do my best to keep a rational mind when I am limit-setting, as I am a more effective leader when I take in the information and respond in a calm and collected manner.

It is much harder to keep the rational mind working when we are in a disagreement or confrontation with a close family member, as our strongest emotional attachments are to our loved ones. If you want to do your best at being a parent or partner, it helps to respond in an attentive and respectful manner to your loved ones. We are not going to be able to achieve our best every single time, but as there is much room for mistakes in the MORE philosophy, stay open to learning from the times you find yourself emotionally engaged in a negative manner and the interaction did not go well. Whether we are at home or work, at rest or play, we need our rational logical mind. The awareness of this and how we can utilize this aspect of ourselves will assist us in all aspects of our lives.

The Emotional Self

There is no doubt that our "Emotional Intuitive Self" is essential to exceptional living through the philosophy of MORE.

The better we can channel the vital and powerful energy that comes from our emotions, the more resources we have for an exceptional life.

We need our emotional-intuitive self to truly connect with others. There is not much connection with a brick wall or at least not a pleasant connection that we want to repeat. A fortress is not built to connect with the outside world, but rather to protect from it. It is through our emotions that we are able to connect with others.

If I am meeting a new client, creating a connection between us is my first priority. Why would the client want to sit in a room with me and tell me private things if they did not feel a connection with me? I will be warm, friendly, and looking for the points of connection, but at the same time, my Informant will be in full swing because I need to gather as much information as possible to be effective for my clients. My Guard will be present, but it is tucked away so I can connect with this new person and pay attention to the information that is coming my way. This is a balanced approach I am using various parts of myself to create an environment where exceptional things can happen.

Our emotional team has three primary players. They are the Connector ~ the great adventurer; the Reactor ~ the energy source and powerhouse of the whole team; and the ultimate Decision Maker ~ our intuition.

The Emotional Self ~ The Connector

The Connector is the most public player on the Emotional Team. It is the job of the Connector to create community and bring us together with other people. It is through the Connector that we secure a sense of belonging. In order to survive, we must have connections. This is wired into us and is essential for survival. There is power in numbers and the stronger your community, the better your chances to thrive. Throughout human history there has been security in connections. A socially isolated person is more vulnerable to bullying and exploitation, just as our distant ancestors were more vulnerable to death from predators or exposure if unprotected.

Since we are vulnerable as a species, we have always needed to form communities to protect ourselves against the elements and dangers in our environment. These communities were based on mutual survival and protection. In prehistoric days, humans would not have survived if they had not banded together. We are not that well-constructed physically for protection. We do not have much hair, we have no shell, and our vital organs are easily exposed to damage. It simply does not take a lot of effort to harm a human being. Our big brain has always been our advantage, but even our greatest asset is not that well protected by our skull. Our bodies cannot sufficiently protect us, so the Connector assists in creating security by bonding us together.

The Connector brings us a lot of pleasure and one of the great gifts of this aspect of our emotional self is love. Romantic love is essential to humans. Not only are our hormones involved as we experience the physical rush of attraction and desire, but we also feel the excitement of sharing ourselves with another and falling in love. The Connector thrives in this love and excitement. Therefore, the combination of a physical attraction that makes us desire proximity with another, combined with the desire to be seen and understood by this same person reaches into our yearning for intimacy.

Romantic love can lead toward the ultimate creative acts of human development, those of pregnancy and childbirth. The Connector is in full swing here, especially since human infants are too vulnerable to survive without nurturance and it is essential that parents and other adults be bonded to children in order for the survival of the human race.

Overall, the Connector has one of the most important jobs imaginable. Basically, the future of the human race rests upon the Connector's shoulders!

The Connector is consistently looking for closeness and

warmth. It is also through the Connector that we develop compassion and caring for others. However, to have true compassion and empathy, we have to be able to access our own vulnerability; and we need to have experienced pain to understand the pain of another. This makes us human. Our emotions and vulnerability have always created the bonds that connect us. If we have sealed away all our vulnerability behind a castle wall, there will be no way to connect, and the human race would not continue. Our rational mind protects and informs us, but it is our intuitive-emotional self that connects us and keeps this whole human thing moving.

It is not just necessity that bonds us—we also feel good when we are around each other. In essence, it is the Connector's job to keep us close to others. The Connector thrives on community and wants to be a part of the big picture. The Connector is fueled by love and feels most satiated by an intimate connection with another person, but is also capable of bringing empathy and compassion to others.

Our parasympathetic nervous system runs our emotions. This is a very powerful system in our body. By activating our emotions, we call on a great deal of energy. Now that we are drawing upon energy, it is time to introduce another member of the team who produces the power behind the actions.

The Emotional Self ~ The Reactor

The Reactor is a strong member of the Emotional team, but as in any chemical reaction, the tremendous power and energy in an emotional reaction creates change and movement.

This energy can be utilized in a highly constructive manner and it fuels the Connector, but at times this energy can also become destructive. There are not a lot of feelings that can beat love, joy, and excitement. These feelings hit the pleasure centres of our brain and produce very pleasant and strong chemical reactions. Our Connector loves these feelings and looks to access the joy and happiness that can bring us close to another human being or a community. But our Reactor is the source of energy and, like any powerhouse; it can facilitate an energy burst that creates movement, either through bringing things together or by blowing them apart.

Along with the pleasurable feelings also come sadness, anger, and frustration, which can cause a lot of disruption, but if managed well, the Reactor can propel tremendous growth. There is a great deal of research that suggests that negative thoughts and negative statements carry more power than positive statements. There is no doubt that dwelling on something destructive seems to make it more powerful. Our Reactor loves the powerful feelings so it will dwell on the pain from our perceived hurts if left unharnessed.

The Reactor can be helpful when it alerts us to the fact that somebody has hurt our feelings or crossed a boundary, but sometimes the Reactor does not discern emotions and it does not want to stop creating energy. It wants more of those powerful charges that come from the parasympathetic nervous system, and will dive right into the deep end to get that charge.

I am not a believer in negative and positive emotions; it is my premise that emotions are neither good nor bad, but that each serves a purpose. Emotions can be useful; however, if there is no movement the emotion can become useless or destructive. If the Reactor does not have a channel for the energy, it can get stuck and dwell on the emotions that disconnect us. This can occur to the point where an emotion spins in on itself with such a ferocious energy that it results in a meltdown. Then the Reactor is no longer a source of energy that creates growth and brings light, but rather a source of destruction and even devastation.

Anger

Many people try to avoid conflict and see anger as a negative emotion. However, anger can fuel us and focus our energy. Anger can let us know when a boundary has been crossed. Still, if anger is left unresolved and unmoved it can turn to destructive rage and create meltdowns that can harm others and oneself. There are things in this world that we should be angry at, and in order to change them, we need energy and direction. The Reactor can bring us this much-needed energy and help fuel positive change. We need our anger and the movement in the MORE philosophy to keep progressing as humans. When we see something that we know is wrong, or that we feel needs to be different, we can start a movement that creates personal and social change.

The advocacy group MADD (Mothers Against Drunk Driving) is a perfect example of something that started as grief and anger, and turned into a call to action. This very personal experience for one mother became a grassroots movement, eventually growing into part of the popular conscience. It began with a mother who was angry and devastated when a drunk driver killed her child. She didn't let her personal anger stay stuck in reactive rage and bitterness. Instead, this mother turned her loss into a movement that has impacted society and changed how we view drinking and driving. It began with intense pain and anger, but was transformed through action into something that has contributed to helping society.

Without a steady flow of movement, the Reactor can simmer and even explode. Simmering anger and resentment can become bitterness, and I believe that bitterness is one of the least attractive traits in another human being. We do not want to connect with another person who is bitter and angry; it sucks out our energy to the point that we start to avoid that person.

Anger that explodes can hit anybody and anything around it. This can be very frightening to others. Rage can also leave a person feeling drained and embarrassed. When our brain is flooded with rage, our higher reasoning does not work well and we are more likely to say and do things that we regret. Rage can leave a real mess that takes a great deal of work to clean up.

Cathy

In order to understand how the Reactor can cause chaos if left undisciplined let's take a look at Cathy.

Cathy had always been a highly emotional person and described herself as a very sensitive child. She often felt that life was unfair, and when she first attended counselling she seemed to be struggling with many of her close relationships. She was in conflict with every one of her family members, even though family was very important to her. She was warm and loving, but Cathy could not figure out why her life was such a mess.

She had married her high school sweetheart, and had three children. She had always wanted a big family, and grew up very close to her parents and siblings. She also reported that she had a history of showing every emotion she felt. Cathy reported that she was often accused of wearing her heart on her sleeve. When she was happy this worked well, but when she was upset there could be a lot of the wrong kind of drama around her. Cathy reported that she had loved being a Mom, and found great pleasure in being there for her kids. But now she was even struggling in her relationship with all three of her children.

Having married shortly after high school, Cathy had three children right away back to back. She had wanted even more children, but had suffered two miscarriages. After trying for some time for a fourth child, she asked her parents if they would help her and her husband fund in-vitro fertility treatments. As she had always been a sensitive and emotional person, her parents hoped that more children would be the thing that would make her happy. So they funded two attempts at in-vitro fertilization. The treatments did not work and Cathy found herself increasingly emotional and sad. As she seldom held back her emotions, everyone was aware of these feelings, including her three children.

An emotional bombshell dropped on Cathy's life after her third child started kindergarten. Someone contacted her anonymously, saying her husband owed him money. She heard in this phone call that her husband had an active drug problem, and that he was stealing money from his place of employment. This was particularly complicated as her father was her husband's employer. She was unable to control her panic and went to her parents for help, telling them about the strange phone call and the accusations against her husband Dan.

It appeared that this information might have been correct as her husband Dan was subsequently fired from his job. He now hated his father-in-law and blamed his wife for exposing him, especially as she went to her parents rather than to him even before there was proof that the information was accurate.

A family feud was in full swing with Dan's family pitted against Cathy's family. The marriage had always been characterized by loud explosive arguments in which they would both yell obscenities at each other, but now it was progressing to pushing and shoving. Dan wanted to sue his father-in-law for wrongful dismissal, denying that he had stolen any money from the company and insisting that Cathy support him. Her parents had always had concerns about Dan and they were not surprised to hear he might be stealing money from the company. They wanted Cathy to leave her husband, and they were also disappointed in her as she appeared unable to manage her life and her family. Cathy's siblings were angry with her for causing so many family problems, and costing their parents and the family company a considerable amount of money.

The arguments between Dan and Cathy escalated and often took place in front of the children or anybody else that was around. Cathy felt she hated her husband and her life. She believed she had done everything to protect her children, but now even her children were disrespectful to her and would not listen to what she said. She was always arguing with her parents as well, since she was still living with Dan.

After one particularly explosive fight, Cathy's husband moved out and she found herself in the position of single Mom. She felt that everyone had let her down and she was caught in a storm of rage and disappointment. In essence, her Reactor was in full swing, and she was experiencing constant meltdowns and a whirlwind of emotions every day that she was having trouble managing. Her doctor prescribed anti-anxiety medication and recommended she attend counselling at my office.

Initially she was resistant to owning any of the problems in her life and wanted to blame everyone else. As long as the Reactor stayed in charge, she did not have to change, and she could feel sorry for herself. There was no doubt she had a lot of legitimate reasons for all her feelings, but she was not making any movement. With the help of counselling she began to identify the places where she was stuck and found techniques to become more aware of her emotions and began taking responsibility for her own life. She became less reactive, and got back to the Connector inside herself who loved the people in her life.

Eventually she and Dan did divorce, and she had very little contact with him as he was still highly reactive in his life and wanted to blame her for all his problems. She healed the wounds with the rest of her family, but also learned how to draw healthy boundaries with the people in her life. She attended counselling with her children and improved her relationship with each of them, helping them access the resources they needed in order to deal with the complex situations in their lives.

In the end, she gained a greater sense of herself rather than just defining herself as mother, daughter, wife, sister, and friend. Cathy is still single and is only now contemplating dating again. She feels that her emotions no longer rule her and she enjoys the connection with others more than ever.

The Emotional Self ~ The Decision Maker

In finding a balance between the emotional and the rational, there is another member of the emotional-intuitive team who is at the centre of everything and, although recognized as important, is often misunderstood. Although we need our rational side to send in the Informant in order to gather information, and our Analyst to organize that information, it is ultimately not the job of the rational mind to make the decision; rather, it is our emotional-intuitive self who is "The Decision Maker." In the end, it is our intuition that is our best guide and makes the best decisions for us.

When we try to make decisions with only our rational mind we can spin in circles and get confused by all the information. Our intuition will approach this decision in a much simpler and more direct manner. We need our intuition to find our way.

When it comes to an important decision, I will gather as much information as I can and look at the situation from all sides. Still, sometimes I can get lost in all this information. Although it was difficult at first, I have learned that, if I let go of the information and "sleep on it," the answer or direction often comes to me the next day.

This is not about a right or wrong decision, but rather a decision that is true to who you are and aligned with your values and sense of self. If things did not unfold as you hoped, it might still have been the experience you needed to have. Our intuition seems to know what life lessons we need and which path will lead us there.

When a decision has been made and a consequence has been suffered, there is often a pattern that is recognized. In situations where the decision has been very costly almost everyone I have spoken with has said that, on recollection, there was some awareness that they were going against their intuition, but for some reason they went ahead and did it anyway.

For example, my daughter had a hard lesson regarding decisions at a young age. She was a naturally curious six year old who enjoyed conducting a variety of science experiments at school and home. Unbeknownst to me, this curiosity had extended to some creation she had placed in ice cube trays and frozen in our freezer. One morning she was determined to get her frozen creation out of the ice cube trays she had used. I was in my room doing my morning routine when this budding scientist decided to remove the frozen material, but she did not know how to get it out of the tray so she grabbed a big butcher knife from the kitchen drawer and decided to pry her concoction out of the tray. Although this was a creative and determined solution, it was also a highly dangerous one for a six year old.

You can imagine the result and how it all came to light to me as I was busy preparing for work and she walked in my room white as a ghost holding her hand. I looked down at her hands that were cupped together and they were filled with blood. After my initial feeling of the room swaying, I was able to get it together enough to examine what had occurred. She had cut into the nail bed of her left thumb.

Of course the aftermath of this science experiment resulted in a trip to the doctor and some emergency treatment. Although I was overwhelmed I knew my role was to tuck in my Reactor and stay calm in order to help my daughter. After it was treated and she told me how the injury had occurred, I asked her what she felt just before she used the knife. She said she knew it was not the right thing to do and she should have waited for me. I did not berate her, or lecture her, but rather I told her that voice inside had been her intuition telling her that waiting was the best decision. I told her that everyone messes up and goes against their intuition once in a while.

I did not feel the need to remove all knives from the house, as I understood this was a learning opportunity for her. I told her she was actually rather lucky as she would have the coolest reminder of her intuition built right into her body. I explained that she would have a ridge on her thumb for the rest of her life and she would just have to rub it when she needed to remind herself to pay attention to her intuition when making a decision.

Yes, there are consequences when we do not listen to our Decision Maker. Not everybody will be as "lucky" as my daughter to have the intuitive reminder built into their body. Despite their intuitive warnings people want what they want and they will often let the Reactor make the decision and go ahead and quit the job, have the affair, or drop out of school. Above all, the saddest compromise of intuition I have witnessed is the pattern I have seen in working with cases of sexual or physical abuse.

Diane

I will never forget the family that I worked with in the aftermath of a sexual abuse allegation, criminal charge and subsequent trial. I have seldom seen the depth of suffering that I witnessed when I provided support to this mother and her children. The mother, Diane, knew she had dismissed her intuition and that as a result her children were deeply hurt. Diane shared her story with me when she sought counselling to assist herself and her children in healing from this devastating situation.

Diane's shocking "reality check" came on a day when she was excited to spend some time with just her daughter. Her children were out of school on a professional day and her son was at a friend's for the day so it was a perfect opportunity to have some "girl time" with her ten year old daughter Katie. It was during that morning, which had initially started out so well, that her daughter disclosed that her stepfather of one year was sexually abusing her.

Diane was stunned by this disclosure, but acted appropriately by telling her daughter that she believed her and that it was the right thing for Katie to tell her mother what had happened. She then took her daughter to the police station and reassured Katie that she would not be hurt by her stepfather again, and that Katie would need to tell some more people what had happened. The police took the girl's statement, and she was sent to the hospital for examination. The police felt they had strong enough evidence to make an arrest that day; they arrested the stepfather when he returned from work that evening. He was charged and eventually found guilty in court.

In working with this family, and through helping Diane and her children heal, I learned many great lessons. Diane told me during a truly honest conversation in counselling that she realized she had always felt something was wrong.

Everything was too perfect. She had been introduced by mutual friends to this man—he was handsome, well off, and had never been married. Her rational mind told her he was kind, sociable, and hardworking. The Informant had gathered a lot of information and the Guard had let him through, but her intuition kept telling her that he seemed too perfect to be true. She went ahead despite these "unreasonable" inner warnings that something was wrong and out of place, and she still married him. Her Informant could not find proof, so she ignored her intuition.

Why did she ignore her intuition? What led her to this compromise? Diane deeply regretted her divorce from the children's father, her first husband. She had always wanted an intact family for her children and her new husband seemed highly supportive of her as a mother and a professional. He was always willing to help take the kids to activities and spend time with her children. She was an intelligent and caring woman, and had never considered herself naive. Nevertheless, she continued to dismiss her intuition, because she deeply wanted an intact family, he seemed "perfect," and she could not find any rational reason for not dating or marrying him.

We often compromise our intuition due to an ideal, rather than truly paying attention and accepting the reality. This was the case with Diane.

There is much wisdom in the saying that if something is too good to be true it probably is. After the disclosure of abuse and through the legal proceedings, the family worked hard in counselling to heal from this heartbreaking situation. It was a painful time for them all, but I was very inspired by Diane who did not hide in her guilt or live only in regret. Rather she used her considerable courage helping her daughter and son to heal. She had made a huge mistake, and it had all started when she ignored her intuition. She was also willing to do whatever she could to heal herself and her children, and faced her compromise head on.

Not many of us have to face a consequence this big, but it is a reminder to pay attention to our intuition and know that it is not our rational mind that should be making the decisions, but that our intuition is the true Decision Maker.

So as stated at the beginning of this chapter, we need all the different aspects of our personality to bring balance and resources to our lives.

At the centre of our teeter totter is the fulcrum between our emotions and logic, and it is here we have access to all the different aspects of ourselves. Our fulcrum knows when to pull forth and when to tuck away, and is formed through time, experience, and learning from our mistakes. This centre of our self is built on resiliency. Once we have taken a few hits and know we can bounce back, we begin to learn how to use our teeter totter to find balance. We might guard in new situations, but we also want to connect with the people we are meeting. We can use both sides of ourselves at the same time should the situation require that from us.

This is not a "one or the other" situation. We can move our different sides forwards and backwards, creating balance as we go and in response to the world around us. A well-functioning teeter totter lets us access all our resources. These two sides of the self are only a problem if an aspect is heavily weighted to one side or the other. For instance, if someone is heavily guarded and cold, they will isolate themselves; if they are heavily reactive and emotional, they will drive others away. The beauty comes in the ability to pull on all aspects of the self as needed. In the end, through experience and awareness, we develop a more effective system that is vibrant, alive, and responsive.

Balance is the main theme in creating an effective teeter totter, as it brings forth different aspects of our rational-logical self and our emotional-intuitive self when we need them. Our rational self has a Guard to protect us, an Informant to gather information, and an Analyst to organize information. When we have a well-developed rational mind we can pull on all these aspects of our logic in the right situation. Still, we also need our emotional-intuitive side to live a fulfilled and connected life. Our emotions are our life force, bringing color and passion to our world. The Connector will take us on great adventures and bring us together with others, and the Reactor will fuel us with active emotions; but it is the Decision Maker who leads us on the exceptional journey. With the MORE philosophy moving us through the reality of the opportunities that our emotional and rational selves present us, our exceptional journeys can create exceptional lives.

Questions for Contemplation

Do you feel you have a strong fulcrum that can pull on both your rational and emotional sides?

Is there a time your Guard has served you well?

Is there a time your Guard has got in the way?

What are you curious about?

Do you get overwhelmed by too much information?

When you think about your life, do you see patterns emerging?

Do you spend time thinking about your life and trying to understand the big picture?

Are you able to put the information away and sleep on it when you need to make a decision?

Who do you feel connected to?

How do you feel when you meet new people?

How do you feel in an unfamiliar situation?

Has your Reactor ever created chaos for you?

Has your anger been a call to action for you?

What emotions energize you?

Have you ever gone against your intuition, and if so what was the outcome?

Are you able to distinguish between your anxiety and your intuition?

Do you think you make your decisions with your rational mind or your intuition?

CHAPTER 10

Anchor Your Relationships to your Purpose and Passion; Go Big and Go Home.

"If an exceptional life is well lived, you really only need one life."

An exceptional life will not look the same for each person; the road to the exceptional life is one that is unique to each individual. The MORE philosophy understands how important it is to be unique and risk being different, thus it has "Exception" as one of its four principles. Each of us needs to be realistic about who we are and then be willing to bring this unique self into the world. Only you can do this. It is in this place of being true to ourselves that we can be true to others, and really bring forth what we have to give. It is also from this place where we can most genuinely experience our own life.

There are concrete steps for each of us to take to move toward our exceptional life, but MORE is not a one-size-fits-all plan that tells you exactly what your life has to look like in order for it to be exceptional. This book has outlined steps to living an exceptional life, but which steps you take to get there are for you to decide and determine. There are many self-help books out there telling you exactly what you need to do and what your life should look like, but this approach is different. Sometimes those books and those experts undermine confidence. If we approach life in a "cookie cutter" way, we limit creativity and passion. You are the best person to determine your own life plan. Your intuition is still the best guide you have, although some guidance from trusted advisors can be of assistance along the way.

This book has focused on the practical side of self-growth and has been committed to telling you the real story. The MORE philosophy is not a "feel good, all is well in the universe" approach, nor is it an "expert has all the answers" approach. This life is not an easy journey, so we need to stop looking for the easy fix-it-all solutions. To me that is a waste of precious time.

This is your life—and it would be sad to think that you are wasting your life looking for a life. Use your common sense and live the life you have! It is important to understand that if a life is well lived, you really only need one lifetime. I believe this is the only lifetime for me that I am aware of and I intend to continue to make it an exceptional life. The MORE philosophy can remind you to make good use of your time on this planet, while allowing yourself to inspire and touch the lives of others as you "live your life to eleven!" Dig into your life and don't be afraid to commit to it and take some risks.

This chapter is going to assist you in understanding how the concept of "go big and go home" applies to you. Essentially, "go big" is your purpose and passion, and "go home" is your anchor and relationships. The MORE philosophy is not a go big or go home approach. An exceptional life is a life where you have passion and purpose that is meaningful to you, plus rich and rewarding relationships with others.

But can we have it all? Can we feel successful in our lives as we stretch out and pursue our purpose, and still connect with others and have successful relationships? Can we experience passion in our relationships and our work?

These are the questions that so many struggle with daily in our modern world. We want to be satisfied and significant, and live a life that matters. The MORE philosophy is a guide to embracing and being present in the opportunities and experiences around us.

Recently, there has been a lot of attention given to the struggle to find an effective life-work balance. Although this is a very real struggle for many people, if we are true to ourselves and are able to pull on the different aspects of our identity as I described in Chapters Eight and Nine, then we can overcome this struggle by being the same person experiencing our life wherever we go and whomever we are with. It is not a question of choosing your home life or your work life. Rather it is about the choices we make with our time. We can feel great satisfaction and success in all aspects of our lives, as well as frustrations and disappointments, but the reality check is that there will be some opportunities taken and some opportunities missed. Again, there is no way around this. We cannot have every opportunity and every experience, but we can manage the choices about which opportunities and experiences we allow into our lives.

All in all, life can feel amazingly full in both the quiet comfortable moments and the big extravagant moments. There really is a vast playing field when we are able to bring ourselves to the game and we are willing to play. We also have to take some quiet moments to understand and study the game, and learn from those around us. Becoming a master at anything is a combination of practice, passion, and patience. To become a master at your exceptional life you will need to utilize all of these qualities.

And now for the biggest and most important reality check of all. It is also an essential step to exceptional living.

Step #14 ~ Accept that You Too Will Die.

It's a reality that we will miss some opportunities, as our time is limited in this world. As much as we do not want to accept it, the blunt truth is that we all eventually die. If we do not understand and accept the inevitability that our time on this planet is limited, then we are living life at a "two" rather than an "eleven." This is it folks! Accept it, and start to live it! So what do we really have when we are here? We have our bodies, our special unique personality, our choices and opportunities, our senses and experiences of the world, and our connections with others. We have our innate unique talents and also the talents and experiences we develop as we live this life.

The topic of death is not a comfortable one, but it is important that we begin having honest conversations regarding this taboo subject. We tend to try to soften the conversations by using words like "passed on" or "is no longer with us," but those conversations skirt the truth and do not really help us as we grapple with the existential truth that we are all going to die one day.

If we could start having honest conversations about death, maybe we could start living life more effectively. It is around the ages of five and six that the prefrontal cortex of our brain develops to the point that we understand death and realize that we, as well as our loved ones, will someday die. It is often a very difficult time for children when they develop the capacity for existential thought. Once we know we can die, we can never erase this knowledge. It is natural to fear death, and the knowledge of our own death haunts us.

As explored in earlier chapters, people spend a lot of time distracting themselves from pain and their fear of death. We also know that love and loss are mingled together.

I cannot remember the exact moment I became aware of death, but I do remember the world changing when I understood that I was not going to be here forever. As a child I could not imagine a world without me or the people I loved. As I became aware of mortality I remember lying in bed at night and thinking about life, death, and the meaning of it all. I would get such a strange disconnected feeling in my body, especially when I thought about a world in which I no longer existed.

As children most of us go through a period where we want to live forever–but as we mature we accept that this will not occur. As we grow older and start to experience real losses, our understanding of death grows as we do. We lose pets, grandparents, aunts, uncles, cousins, friends and parents, and we realize that death is not going to go away. I have come to understand that accepting death is necessary in order to live an exceptional life. This inevitability makes us pay attention to the gift that life is. We would never appreciate this experience if we did not understand the value of time and our choices with our time.

Our time is limited, so when I say "go big and go home" I am encouraging you to be conscious of your time and understand that you do not have to live half a life. I am encouraging you to grab your life firmly and dig deeper into it. Do not waste much time with fear and avoidance.

How do we manage time in this limited life? There is no doubt in my mind that the most important and valuable assets I have are the connections and moments I have with the people I love; these most important assets deserve the highest priority. This will require a commitment of attention to those meaningful moments. Big feelings can come in small moments. Nothing beats those small moments of affection such as a hug from my son, a smile from my daughter, a laugh with my nephew, and the moments I braid my niece's hair. Breathe in those moments and get back in your body so you can experience yourself and the relationship. Those are the moments to take personal and hold close to your heart.

To manage our time well, we need to pay attention to which relationships nourish us and assist us in better experiencing our lives. Are we uplifted in some way by this experience or person, and do we feel excited by what we have to contribute? Can I be "real" with this person, or do I feel disconnected?

Stop wasting time on people or experiences that drag you down. Look to that which elevates you. Stop lying to yourself if you already know that you are in something that devalues you in some way. If it is a difficult relationship, is there something for you to learn from this experience, or is it just the same old spinning going nowhere?

Your choices should bring movement and value into your life. If you are not feeling this, you may not be making the best choices with your time. There is no benefit to you, others, or the world if you are stuck and disconnected. Ask yourself what people and what experiences bring gratitude and purpose into your life. These are the places to invest your time.

I have had both the fortune and misfortune of a true

life-and-death scare—this certainly reminded me of the time limit in my life. I share this most personal of moments to illustrate how we need to pay attention to the wake-up calls, and to focus on gratitude for this life. It is also the moment that helped me define much of what is written in this book. A couple of years ago I had a health emergency that brought many things to light for me, and also illustrated the depth of connection with those I love.

It was a morning just like most other mornings. After a restful sleep, I felt great when I readied myself for a productive day at the office. There was absolutely no warning that anything was wrong. I felt vital and energetic and all was well in my world. But after settling into my desk and beginning my morning tasks, I felt an overpowering nausea. I had never felt anything like it before in my life. Within minutes, I was in shock as I was throwing up blood. I was rushed to the hospital. I will not get too gory at this part, but for those who saw the original movie Carrie based on a Stephen King novel, some images might come to mind!

An artery had burst in my stomach wall and I was experiencing a full-on gastrointestinal bleed. I have now learned that an artery pumps a lot of blood very quickly, so there was no arguing about the seriousness of what was happening to me. I lay on the gurney at the hospital quickly losing blood, but also beginning to feel a strange peace.

Part of this peace might have come from the fact that my blood pressure was dropping quickly and my brain was not getting the oxygen it needed. But not wanting to question this gift, I allowed the peace to spread through me. I could no longer articulate words, but I was still conscious. I knew I was in the hospital and the doctors were doing what they needed to do, so I did not feel afraid.

I looked at my husband who was standing close by, and although he looked like he was going to pass out any second, I just held his eyes and attempted to communicate love and appreciation into that look. I also knew that if I died, I was not leaving anything unsaid or unresolved. My life had been exceptional up to that moment–I knew that inside. I also knew that I did not feel ready to let go and that I still wanted more of this life. I wanted the movement, the opportunity, and the reality of this exceptional life to continue. It actually surprised me that my dominant feeling was one of satisfaction and gratitude for the amazing life and connections I had. I knew with certainty that the moments of connection were the most precious things in my life.

As luck and medical intervention would have it, I was treated quickly and have been given more time in this amazing world, and a real life experience that reminds me to stay grateful!

At some level, this whole book is about that moment; that moment of realizing how exceptional life is and how grateful I am for the relationships in my life. It was such an unexpected crisis and although there is a thought at the back of my mind that something unexpected could happen again I do not live in fear of it. I actually view my health crisis as an amazing gift and a very effective reality check.

If life gives you a hard knock, I encourage you to be careful about how much time you waste feeling sorry for yourself. Limit it to as little time as possible and then move forward. If you can limit the "Oh, poor me!" time to fifteen minutes, you will be using your time wisely. It is human and natural to feel sorry for oneself, just be conscious of the time spent doing so. I encourage you, even on your worst day, to remind yourself that it is a privilege to be in the real world and to have the opportunity to live this exceptional life.

Remain aware that the moments of connection between people are what matter the most. Nevertheless, we do not need to devote every breathing moment to communication and sharing space with one another.

I believe we need to pay attention and to be present in those moments, but we also need to spend time with ourselves. Even if you are social and find people invigorating, you will benefit from quiet time to recharge, contemplate, and be creative. Other people, even those we love the most, can become distracting. If you spend all your time focused on your family and close relationships, and build your sole purpose in life around them, you may find that you actually lose appreciation for each other and lose yourself somewhere along the way. It pays to remember that sometimes it feels good to leave home in order to just experience the joy of coming home again. If we never say goodbye we never get the joy of a hello.

That brings us back to the struggle with the balance between work and home. Again, I see this as a balance between choices and opportunities, not as a choice between one or the other. As people forge ahead in their lives, trying to meet expectations and pressures, they end up overwhelmed, exhausted, and not feeling particularly efficient anywhere in their lives. I have talked to those who feel they cannot do it all, that they have to choose between home and work. This can lead to the feeling that one has to "go big or go home." I understand that this saying has become an encouragement of sorts, so that one shows up to the challenges in life and gives it their all. I do agree we need to show up, and that we need to be prepared for some risks. We need to learn how to grieve the opportunities we let pass and embrace the opportunities we choose to pursue.

But I also believe that the recipe for success is that we need to pursue our passions, as well as secure ourselves in the world. All in all, we need our purpose to keep us passionate and our anchor to keep us secure.

Living an authentic life also reduces exhaustion. It can be truly draining to have to put on a face in order to "go big" to the world and then only have your true self emerge at home. Those who are successful and living exceptional lives are authentic at both home and work. We need to fly in this world, but we also need an anchor. We all know what happens to a kite on a windy day if nobody is holding it, and what happens to a boat in water without an anchor. We also know that an anchor without a boat is just something stuck in the mud and a kite without a hand holding it is just something stuck in a tree. We can find our purpose when we are safely anchored and we can fuel success when we are secure and living with passion in all areas of our lives.

As I was raising my family, I saw many mothers and fathers struggle with how to balance all their responsibilities. I also saw a generation of people who wanted it all, but ended up feeling stressed, guilty, and unfulfilled. How do I pursue my passions and be the committed parent or partner that I want to be? How do I have a sense of self that is not solely defined by what I do for a living or who I am in a relationship with?

Step #15 ~ Give Up Idealism and Become a Realistic Optimist

Realistic Optimism

There is a certain disillusionment that comes when we realize that our time and resources are limited. This is all part of maturity, but this disillusionment does not mean we cannot live an exceptional life. In order to deal with reality and follow the steps of the MORE philosophy, we need to become disenchanted with our dreams and superficial desires, so that we can sink our teeth into the real world. It is only within the real world that we can experience real satisfaction.

There will be things we need to compromise, but rather than suffer from guilt and disappointment, the best compromise is to release the idealism with as much grace as possible and move toward realistic optimism. If we stay idealistic and do not pay attention to the reality checks, we will not be truly present in our lives. If we become pessimistic and disappointed in our lives, we will harden up and disconnect. Conclusively, these are both lose-lose situations.

In my practice, I have seen many people struggle with accepting that life had not turned out the way they wanted. They were disappointed with their marriage, their parents, their friendships, their jobs, their children, and their own parenting. It struck me that the most disillusioned people I met were the ones who based their choices on a romantic and idealistic view of the world. Each decision was approached with such good intentions and great hopes. This was going to be the best marriage, the best friend, the best job, the best child, and the best experience ever. They had started out so high and fell so far.

Then, there were the pessimists who only saw failure and disappointment. A pessimist views the world through a negative frame. They might be great at reality checks, but they are also great at deflating a situation or idea. They can predict all the problems right from the start and then feel vindicated when their predictions come true. For example, they might believe that their marriage will never work, their friends never cared, their job sucks, and people don't listen to them. A pessimist is often critical and harsh and, from my experience, a person that you find yourself avoiding because they are just such a "drag" to be around.

Over time, I realized that there had to be a middle ground between idealism and pessimism, as both lead to unexceptional lives. There needed to be an approach that is based in reality, but still encourages positive growth and movement. I coined the phrase "Realistic Optimism," because "optimism" moves us forward and provides positive options, and "reality" gives us the direction and information needed to achieve our goals.

When operating from the reality check of the MORE philosophy, we can feel disappointment and sadness, yet still hold onto a positive vision, a "diamond in the mind" that we can work toward. The MORE philosophy asks the individual to have a certain level of trust in the bigger picture. If you open up to the possibilities, then life will move you toward the diamond, although it might not always look the way you had hoped or anticipated. In fact, there is often freedom in letting go of hope, if the hope is just based in idealism.

I have another saying that sounds rather pessimistic, but

actually it is Realistic Optimism. It is, "Once you give up hope, things get better."

Sometimes idealistic hope can keep a person away from the real possibilities in their life. I have seen many people hang onto hope and dig deeper into denial. I am not saying that there is no place for hope; however, there are some kinds of hope that can be destructive if you end up living your life in anticipation of the hope being achieved, and therefore missing out on the life that is right in front of you. If the thing you hope for is unattainable or based on some perfectionistic vision, your whole life could slip by if you don't let go of that hope. Magic and miracles may occur, but if one is basing their well-being on a miracle occurring, that is a pretty big gamble. I would rather bet on reality, as I know the real world exits. Optimistic Realism is the path to a life that is far more fulfilling and interesting than the dreams or fears we have.

Step #16 ~ Move Purpose and Passion in the Same Direction

When people feel they have to choose between personal passion and personal connections, the choice undermines their ability to live an exceptional life. I have seen many of my friends and clients beat themselves up when they felt that they have not been a good enough parent, wife, or even child.

The other side of the dilemma occurs to people who feel that they are being pulled in two different directions at once; that in order to commit to their relationships; they have to compromise their personal passions and interests.

Another step to an exceptional life is the acceptance and understanding that one does not have to go in two different directions, and that one's purpose and anchor are connected and come from the same place, and combined, they move us in the same direction. The danger of relationships and personal purpose going in opposing directions is that you might attach yourself to only your work role or your home role. This can lead to a very weak sense of self. Without a strong sense of self we often feel unfulfilled and unseen.

We may feel some significance in the roles we play, but if this significance is defined through who you are to others, then you might lose your sense of self when the relationship changes in some way. I have seen this when a parent makes their children the prime focus of their lives–the parent can then feel lost and unimportant when the children become more independent. This is different than making your children a priority, as a priority is about responsibility and care whereas prime focus becomes about defining oneself through the relationships with others.

Go big and go home is about acquiring a sense of purpose in life and a sense of being a unique person who is making his own mark in the world anchored from a place of belonging and significance. There are many people who only define themselves through their roles or their jobs, and both of these avenues can lead to disappointment and problems. Go big and go home is about aligning your personal purpose with your personal relationships, acknowledging that time is precious and important, and then choosing where to put your time and attention.

Passion can be found in many areas of our life. In our work, play, sports, art, books, music, business, creative pursuits, conversations, and whatever else gets you excited in life. One can have purpose and passion in their interests and their relationships. We all need to be able to anchor ourselves in the real world and we can bring our "home" with us out into the rest of the world. If we are satiated and filled up within our personal relationships we can go out into the world with energy and excitement. It is like eating a healthy breakfast, and then facing the day. If we go out into the world hungry and ungrounded, we are more vulnerable and have less energy.

It is also essential to be able to bring the world back to our relationships, as this keeps things vibrant and moving. If the go big never goes home, our relationships become stagnant. As movement is one of the main principles of the MORE philosophy it is best to have this flow of energy and information in both our "work" and our "home."

In fact, if we are not well-anchored at home, it is pretty difficult and unfulfilling to go big. It is when we have an anchor and a sanctuary in the world that we can feel free to take risks and explore new opportunities. When we feel secure and connected with those we love, and we have a refuge from the world, we can pull on our courage to take chances and make an impact in the world. If we are just living for the moments outside our "home," without the grounding and security of our relationships then life becomes only a performance where we are wearing one role or another. The result of too much performing is that it leads to people feeling fake and inauthentic in their own lives.

To have a life that goes to eleven you need to be the main character in your own story and be present for its highs and lows. The "go home" is the place where we can collect ourselves and our valued relationships so that we can shine in the rest of the world. It is also the place we can rest and relax, and simply be ourselves, and recover when we need to.

Essentially, it all starts at home. This is where our early development begins and where we develop the template for our life. Our early experiences shape our lives and attachments and how we perceive the world around us.

Although I am a parent and passionate about my children and my parenting, I am not someone who believes that a person must have children to be fulfilled. But family is important, and we have all come from a family that shaped us to some extent. Our family experiences will be different from one another, but family is part of us all. Even if you do not have a partner or children, or your life is in transition, your experiences and connections live within you at all times. If one is living alone, or living with a house full of people, one still needs to find a way to be anchored and able to collect oneself at "home."

Purpose

I recall a night many years ago before I had children, when we were invited to dinner at a friend's home and were enjoying some after-dinner conversation. I always love to play "table games" with people where we ask questions and have conversations at the dinner table. I asked the couple we were visiting what they felt their prime purpose in the world was. My friends had two children aged five and seven at the time, and my one friend immediately replied that her purpose in the world was her children. I struggled with this answer.

Although I was not a mother yet, her answer left me unsettled. I thought my discomfort might have been due to the fact that I was not a parent, and I would possibly feel as she did if I became a parent in the future, although I doubted this. Eventually I did become a parent and I still thought about her answer. Did I feel my children were my prime purpose in life? Was my role as their mother the thing that truly defined me? I did feel parenting was my most important job and I was passionate about my children, but the truth was that I did not feel it was my purpose.

I feel that parenting is my responsibility, but I do not feel that my role of mother or wife or daughter is my purpose. I do not feel my role of counsellor or teacher, author or business woman is my purpose. My purpose does not feel as though it can be defined by a role, any role in my life. I value and appreciate all my roles, but my purpose feels different. It is that unique part that is me that I can choose to contribute to any situation or person in my life. Therefore, my purpose is never limited by my roles or my environment. Ultimately, my purpose comprises the contributions and perspectives that I uniquely bring to the table. This is the exceptional part of the MORE philosophy that allows me to go big and go home, because my unique self and purpose move with me everywhere I go.

Now that my children are growing and moving forward in their own lives, I am even more convinced of this. We get in trouble and stuck when our purpose rests on somebody else's shoulders; if my purpose in this world were my children, then my purpose certainly could become a burden to them and weigh heavily on their shoulders. My go big is my passion and my own purpose, and although our lives and passions are woven together, my children will have their own purposes to discover.

My children will always be a part of my go home and go big, as they are part of my anchor and my passion. I will also be a part of their anchors, as they pursue their purposes in the world. As the years progress, they will discover their passions and purpose, and collect other significant relationships, but the template we have set for them will always be a part of their anchor, as the one set for me by my parents is still a part of my grounding and experience of this world. I will contribute to their growth and development, and I do need to do the best job I can at parenting, but their lives are not my purpose and my life is not their purpose. It is my responsibility to understand and define this. You can have a strong, attached, and secure relationship with the people you love, as well as pursue interests and passions in life. In some sense, you really can have it all!

This balance of security and passion brings to mind a time when my daughter was still young and she was trying to understand why her father and I went to work. As I explained it to her, this all became increasingly clear in my mind. I let her know that both she and her brother were always our first priority. I told her that everyone, including her, should contribute the thing they do well to the world, and that my counselling practice was the thing I did well. I reassured her that the members of my family were the people whom I love the most, but that I went to work because it made me feel good to be of assistance to others and I could bring these good feelings home in the same way she could bring her good feelings home from school. I also reminded her she could bring any feeling home and that if she needed help sorting them out, home was a great place to sort out feelings.

In my message to her, I never once said I worked for money to get us things or pay bills. She was a very thoughtful child and she understood what I meant and wondered about what she would contribute when she grew up. I continue to let her know that I am confident she will figure it out and that I have no doubt that she will lead an exceptional life with great contributions to this world. I know in my heart the children in our hearts and home will go big and go home as well.

The Guide

As explored and expanded through this book, the MORE philosophy is made up of the four principles of Movement, Opportunity, Reality, and Exception. Each chapter has mapped out and included steps that you can follow to live an exceptional life. It is my belief that the MORE philosophy can be applied to every situation and relationship, as well as to the quietest and loudest of moments. These steps can lead you on an amazing and interesting journey.

It is also my hope that people will come to understand that counselling can be a great navigational tool that propels us forward in this exceptional life. The MORE approach is not problem-based, but rather uses challenges and problems as the vehicles for growth. You may feel you can get there on your own, and this book may be enough to assist you along the path, but you may also want to consider hiring a guide who can help you navigate your path more quickly and safely. I have always seen counselling as a guided tour illuminating the points of interest along the way. A good guide who is well-informed, practical and familiar with the terrain can be of great assistance.

As a young adult travelling in Australia with my brother and our friend, I had a real life experience that I will share that illustrates how I discovered the value of a good guide. We had taken the beautiful train trip to the rainforest station of Kuranda in North Australia and decided it would be a great experience to spend a couple of hours doing a "jungle walk" before the train returned to Cairns at the end of the day. We saw some signs that were posted that said "Jungle Walk ahead" and off we went to check out the rainforest. We were young, enthusiastic and did not realize that the standard practice for tourists was to hire a specialized guide to go through the jungle. I was on a budget and felt we did not need to spend the money on a guide, as we could navigate it ourselves.

We went into the jungle with the best of intentions and the poorest of preparations. As we were only going to walk through the paths for a couple of hours, we did not even bring a water bottle. To make a long story short, we got totally lost, disoriented, and very thirsty, and spent the entire day trying to get back out of the jungle. We did eventually find our way out and we did do it ourselves, but had we secured a good guide and received the right information it would have been a far safer, far quicker and more pleasant experience. The several hours lost in the jungle filled with fear and panic stay fresh in my mind, and act as a constant reminder of the value of a good guide. We certainly learned some lessons that day and suffered our fair share.

With a good guide you can learn much more quickly and enjoy the journey. I have acted as your guide through this book, and–Yes!–life can feel like a bit of a jungle at times. Through the MORE philosophy, I have pointed out steps toward an exceptional experience, while paying attention to your safety and security. In this way, a guide in a jungle and a counsellor guiding you to understand yourself and your life are very similar.

In conclusion, I believe that the exceptional life is attainable and vibrant, but it is not some evolved state we achieve. It is right here, right now. It is filled with passion and mistakes and movement. There are many opportunities to explore and I encourage you to make your own unique mark in the world. It has been a pleasure to be your guide through this book and I hope that you have found your time well spent. Go ahead and turn up the volume to eleven, even when others tell you the volume of life only goes to ten, and enjoy your exceptional life!

Author Biography

Alyson Jones, MA, RCC, is a highly respected therapist, educator and writer who has practiced and defined a no-nonsense approach to an exceptional life, and is excited to share her insights with you. She is President of a large private counselling centre, Alyson Jones & Associates (alysonjones.ca), where she leads a professional team of therapists who are committed to providing MORE outstanding services to a wide range of clients. She holds a Masters in Counselling Psychology and has practiced as a therapist for over 20 years, working with all age groups. Alyson is prominent in the psychological community and is an Adjunct Faculty member at the Adler School of Professional Psychology in Vancouver, B.C. where she enjoys inspiring her students. Her authentic, enthusiastic personality captivates audiences and she is often invited by the media to share her extensive knowledge. She is regularly featured on programs such as The Bill Good Show, The Simi Sara show and The CKNW Morning News with Philip Till. In addition to her professional life, Alyson lives in North Vancouver with her exceptional family where she enjoys being a wife, mother, sister, aunt, daughter, and friend.

Alyson Jones shares thought-provoking, informative, and entertaining multimedia keynote presentations and workshops at conferences, businesses, schools, and other group settings for both public and professional audiences. As a Child and Family Therapist and Clinical Director at Alyson Jones & Associates, she enthusiastically leads one of the largest counselling centres in the country and is often featured in the media sharing her extensive knowledge. As a speaker, Alyson believes in bringing MORE practical and relevant information to the community. She does this in a no-nonsense practical and humorous way. Her work as clinical director, counsellor, public speaker, parent educator, teacher, and author brings great substance to her presentations; but it is her very human warmth and wit that enables her to touch and inspire the lives of many.

To learn more about Alyson Jones please visit:
www.AlysonJones.ca.

Facebook: Alyson Jones & Associates
Twitter: @MOREAlysonJones
LinkedIn: Alyson Jones & Associates
http://ca.linkedin.com/pub/alyson-jones/30/979/132

If you want to get on the path to be a published author by **Influence Publishing** please go to www.InspireABook.com

Inspiring books that influence change

More information on our other titles and how to submit your own proposal can be found at www.InfluencePublishing.com

CPSIA information can be obtained at www.ICGtesting.com
Printed in the USA
LVOW13s0946111013

356393LV00005B/15/P